UNMASKING
Sexual Con Games
3rd Edition

Unmasking Sexual Con Games, 3rd Ed.

Published by the Boys Town Press
Boys Town, Nebraska 68010

www.girlsandboystown.org/btpress

The Boys Town Press is the publishing division of Girls and Boys Town, the original Father Flanagan's Boys' Home.

The Girls and Boys Town National Hotline is a 24-hour crisis line for parents and children with any problem.

1-800-448-3000

10   9   8   7   6   5   4   3   2   1

UNMASKING
Sexual Con Games
3rd Edition

Helping TEENS Avoid

EMOTIONAL GROOMING and DATING VIOLENCE

by
KATHLEEN M. McGEE
LAURA J. BUDDENBERG

BOYS TOWN PRESS

BOYS TOWN, NEBRASKA

Also from the Boys Town Press

Boundaries: A Guide for Teens

A Good Friend

Who's in the Mirror?

What's Right for Me?

Teaching Social Skills to Youth

Common Sense Parenting®

Common Sense Parenting of Toddlers and Preschoolers

Parenting to Build Character in Your Teen

Angry Kids, Frustrated Parents

Practical Tools for Foster Parents

Rebuilding Children's Lives

Building Skills in High-Risk Families

Skills for Families, Skills for Life

Parenting After September 11, 2001

Dealing with Your Kids' 7 Biggest Troubles

Parents and Kids Talking about School Violence

The Well-Managed Classroom

Safe and Effective Secondary Schools

Treating Youth with DSM-IV Disorders

Common Sense Parenting Learn-at-Home Video Kit

Getting Along with Others

Dangerous Kids

Girls and Boys Town Book on Patriotism

Time to Enrich K-6 Activity Kit

Time to Enrich 7-12 Activity Kit

www.girlsandboystown.org/btpress
For a free Boys Town Press catalog, call 1-800-282-6657

Table of Contents

Introduction

"If you love me, prove it."

"I'm going to make you feel good."

"You want it, you know you do."

"Just this once."

"What's the big deal? Everybody does it."

Language Can be a powerful persuader. The term "con game" (confidence game) is defined as a swindle in which a person is defrauded after his or her confidence has been won.

When someone is tricked into a sexual encounter by what another person says, it is called a "sexual con game." Anyone who is coerced into a sexual experience has been defrauded both emotionally and physically.

This manual examines the kinds of words and behaviors that can be used to seduce, trick, or force teenagers into a sexual relationship. The more educated and aware our youth are about sexual con games, the more they will be able to "unmask" and avoid the con artist.

Depending on the context, the con artist can also be referred to as a "perpetrator," "predator," "player," or "groomer." Other slang terms include "pimp," "G man," "mac daddy," and so on. There may be differences in the intensity of the physical or emotional relationship, but all con artists are guilty of creating coercive relationships. Some con artists knowingly manipulate and convince others to engage in sex. Some simply mimic the actions of the role models they have seen and are unaware of what healthy relationships are. Although these tactics can be used by anyone of any age, we will concentrate on helping teenagers become aware of how others may threaten or damage their healthy moral and sexual development.

This curriculum was first published for use with Girls and Boys Town High School students and taught within the context of a human sexuality and relationship course. Many of these students had been sexually abused and emotionally manipulated by adults or other teenagers before coming to Girls and Boys Town. Due to their backgrounds, they were very familiar with the types of behavior described in this manual, and learned to recognize the ways sexual con artists had taken advantage of them.

Word spread quickly about the success of the curriculum and soon requests for training and materials were coming in from around the country. Teachers, counselors, youth ministers, and parents were finding that the information presented in the *Unmasking Sexual Con Games* curriculum was not only helpful to at-risk youth who had already been emotionally and sexually manipulated, but was also an effective preventive tool for teaching all teens about healthy and unhealthy relationships. Today the *Unmasking Sexual Con Games* materials are used in a variety of settings, from junior high and high school classrooms and church youth groups to detention centers, shelters, and residential group homes.

Sexual con games, harassment, or even sexual abuse can affect youth of any age, attending any school. It is not restricted to age, race, or gender. For example, a national survey conducted by researchers at Wellesley College's Center for Research on Women, published by *Seventeen* magazine and reprinted in *USA Today*, revealed startling rates of sexual harassment in our schools. More than 4,200 female students from grades 2 through 12 responded.

The survey found that of the respondents:

- 39 per cent had been harassed at school every day during the past year.

- 89 per cent had been subjected to sexual comments or gestures.

- 83 per cent had been touched or grabbed.

- When administrators or teachers were informed of the harassment, the school took action in only 55 per cent of the cases.

Many of the respondents also shared their personal experiences at school such as:

"I've been sexually harassed for almost three years. One guy kept trying to feel me up and go down my pants in class. It breaks down your soul and brings you down mentally and physically."

– 14-year-old, New Hampshire

"There was a guy in my art class who thought it was his privilege to grab my butt whenever he wanted. Like a fool, I thought it was just 'flirting' or 'teasing' but it still made me feel dirty and violated. No human being should be subject to such degradation."

– 15-year-old, Texas

"My harassment came from one boy. Constantly. He was really into smacking my bottom, among other things, and always asking me to go to bed with him. I didn't want to go to school."

– 14-year-old, Illinois

"The guys would want you to let them touch you all over. The school and the principal wouldn't listen to me."

– 13-year-old, Kansas

The information in this manual can help teens learn how to deal with people who attempt to harass or coerce them into sexual activity. We cannot turn our backs or close our eyes in the hope that sexual harassment and sexual con games will just "go away." Teenagers will not just "grow out of it." Manipulative boys are not just "being boys." Manipulative girls are not just being "flirts." Somehow, somewhere, many teenagers have lost the innocence of childhood and the joy that comes with healthy relationships. It is our responsibility to teach our teens what is acceptable behavior and what is not. Above all else, we must teach them that sexually using and abusing another person is morally and legally wrong and will not be tolerated.

The material contained in this manual can be a springboard for some very interesting and frank discussions about teenage sexuality. An open, yet disciplined classroom or discussion group can be a valuable forum for teens to learn about their own sexuality and how to avoid being used.

Some of the information in this leader's manual is also included in the Teen's Guide. Adult leaders and teachers should decide how the other information that is presented here should be used. While the content issues presented in the Leader Guide and the Teen's Guide are the same, the wording in some sections may be different. Therefore, it is important that leaders read and become familiar with the material in both manuals before they begin a class.

Suggested lesson plans for leaders can be found in Chapter 10. Included in the lessons are excerpts from actual letters written by teenagers to other teenagers. The letters are used as examples to teach young people to recognize the games played to convince them to have sex. The curriculum is broken down into sessions that focus on specific topics relating to the concepts described in this book. **It is strongly recommended that the information in this manual be used in a single-gender classroom. Many students could be uncomfortable discussing sensitive topics in front of the opposite gender.**

Warning!

Some of the material in this manual is explicit and, therefore, controversial. In particular, some people may find the "grooming letters," included in this manual for teacher reference and as a teaching activity, not appropriate for use with teens. Although many of the letters contain subtle grooming tactics, some contain language that is offensive and vulgar. The letters are not included for shock value, but to show the reality of the language heard and spoken by some of today's teenagers. In some of the letters, the perpetrator's con game will be obvious to adults. However, these same letters, when written to an unsuspecting and vulnerable teen, can be a potent enticement. (The letters are presented with original grammatical and spelling mistakes as well as sexual slang terms in order to retain their authenticity. Some graphic obscenities have been deleted or edited. Names have been changed.)

The manner in which you decide to use the letters and information in this manual is left to your judgment. Please be prudent. Some adult leaders prefer to pick and choose certain sections to use in their classrooms. Some adult leaders choose certain letters but delete any offensive language. Others use the curriculum in its entirety.

When deciding how to implement this curriculum, it's important to consider the age and developmental level of the students. Other crucial concerns could include a school administration's or youth organization's attitude toward the material, parental and community response, and the amount of cooperation adult leaders have from their students' parents.

One of the primary issues, however, centers on your own attitude and openness toward teaching students about exploitive sexual behavior. You have to be comfortable with the material and be able to present it in an open, caring, honest manner, without resorting to "scare tactics" or condemnation. Your intent should be to inform and guide your students, not moralize or preach. If presented properly, this curriculum can help young people learn about the cruel games sexual con artists play and how to avoid being used by such people.

Helping students learn about sexual matters is sometimes a delicate issue. But when the information is presented in an appropriate and sensitive manner, it can empower students with knowledge that will allow them to build healthy relationships and avoid the hurt and shame that results from being sexually used. This must begin with learning how the sexual con artist operates, thus unmasking the groomer's real intentions. Then the game and the groomer lose their power.

Emotional Grooming

When a person manipulates someone's emotions and skill-fully gains control of the target, we call that process "emotional grooming." Emotional grooming is used to seduce, coerce, or "con"

other youth into sexual activity. Grooming is a preparation, a process where the "groomer" – the person who tries to gain control of another person – tries to trick, convince, or coax a target into some form of sexual behavior.

Sometimes, these tactics are deliberately and carefully thought out and planned. Other times, groomers merely mimic what they have seen, heard, and learned from others. In almost all cases, groomers don't know how to create a healthy relationship and usually have a warped and self-centered view of what others can do for them. They most likely learned their behaviors and other misinformation about relationships from peers, media, or adult role models. Most have never seen or experienced the mutual respect and selfless behaviors it takes to create a healthy relationship.

Regardless of the level of culpability, if the groomer is successful, the target usually ends up in a sexually abusive, manipulative relationship. The groomer attempts to control the target both physically and emotionally.

A Coercive Process

The process of emotional grooming can occur at any age. Young people who have not developed distinct and healthy personal boundaries are very vulnerable to a groomer's tactics. Many teens do not fully understand the psychological, emotional, and social impact of engaging in sexual activity. The emotional groomer attempts to teach them that premarital sexual activity is not only acceptable but also expected. The groomer uses seduction, bribes, or threats to teach this "lesson." Although targets may know something is wrong, the groomer establishes and maintains a position of power and authority. Many adolescents who end up in such manipulative relationships were conditioned at an early age to "please" others no matter what. The groomer takes full advantage of this trait. Other targets are so starved for attention, for someone to care for and protect them, that they will ignore or dismiss the physical or emotional coercion and manipulation just to "have" a boyfriend or girlfriend.

Youth who fall prey to emotional grooming are often talked into doing things that are immoral or illegal just to please the groomer. Many times, younger youth become targets because they aren't as physically or emotionally strong or aware of manipulation as adults or older youth. Many youth who are sexually abused are conned into believing that this is the way they should behave. They are told repeatedly that sexual activity is the way to show love, and they believe it. They are convinced that having premarital sex is expected and accepted, and is something they should do to earn love, acceptance, or status.

Learning about the tactics, cons, and lines used by groomers will help youth figure out when someone is trying to use and manipulate them. That's the first step. Teens need to be aware. They need to know how to recognize the groomer's tactics and lines, and then use this knowledge to avoid being used or hurt by others.

The information on emotional grooming is not presented to make youth fearful of being manipulated or abused by everybody. Teens need to realize that there are many good and trustworthy people in their lives who want what's best for them. They cer-tainly can learn to develop healthy and wonderful relationships with other people. But the reality of today's world mandates that we make teens aware that there are some people who are out to please only themselves. We don't want our youth getting emotionally or physically hurt by someone they believed they could trust.

Emotional groomers are manipulators. And some are very skilled. Some groomers will try whatever is necessary to convince a youth of the groomer's undying love and loyalty. Often, the target desperately wants to feel protected and wanted, and this desperation makes the groomer's task even easier. By the time a target feels or realizes that something is wrong, the groomer quite probably has enough control over the target to get what he wants.

Emotional groomers actually are perpe-trators. The word "perpetrate" means to be responsible for carrying out a crime. And that's exactly what sexually taking advantage of another person is – a crime. The emotional groomer is the worst kind of thief. He steals a young person's youthfulness and happiness; she robs young targets of the innocence and safety to which they are entitled. Groomers leave targets confused, humiliated, and ashamed.

The following material is designed to help teens understand how groomers go about emotionally preparing and shaping other people's behavior in order to use them. Teens should understand that the groomer wants control. Teens also need to know that there are ways to avoid these controlling sexual con games. The groomer is skillful in playing the game but that doesn't mean the target is powerless. The more a teen knows about how to recognize sexual con games, the easier it will be to unmask the groomer and see the game for what it really is.

Characteristics of a Groomer

There are no specific physical characteristics that identify an emotional groomer. A groomer could be male or female, teen or adult, a college graduate or a high school dropout. It's what the groomer does and says – his or her behaviors and words – that can alert a teen to the possibility of a con game.

Some people think that since males are typically more sexually aggressive that emotional groomers are always male. It is true that most sexual crimes – rape, sexual assault, and sexual abuse – are perpetrated by males. Yet, there are many females who use sexual con games to manipulate and get what they want. In fact, in some contemporary music and teen movies girls as well as guys are encouraged to be "players." Elements of contemporary youth culture actually glamorize, admire and respect the player. **The important thing to note is that a groomer or a target could be anyone of either gender.**

In order to remind the reader that a target or groomer could be of either gender, the text will vary the use of pronouns when describing both groomers and targets. Sometimes the groomer will be referred to as "he" and sometimes as "she." Likewise, the target will sometimes be referred to as "she" and other times as "he."

Emotional groomers sometimes disguise their con games with what seem to be caring behaviors in order to mask their real intent. For example, friends often give gifts to one another as an expression of how much they care. It makes the giver feel as good as the receiver. That's normal. The groomer, however, gives his target a present because he wants something in return. Every time he does something for his target, he chalks it up as something his target owes him. He runs a system of sexual debits and credits and expects to be paid in full.

Groomers may be "slick" talkers. They may be skilled at intimidating others. They may have "status" at a school or with a group of peers. They may have money or access to drugs or alcohol. Regardless of how they play their con games, groomers take emotional and physical advantage of others.

Why Groomers Groom

How does someone become a groomer? Most often, it is simply a matter of imitating and mimicking observed behavior. Many teens groom because they believe that this is how you're supposed to act in a relationship. This is how you get the guy or girl you want – it's how you prove you're "macho" or "cool." Or, they believe that the purpose of dating is to get sex and the way you get sex is through grooming. Perhaps they've seen grooming "work" for older siblings, parents, or other family members. Perhaps they've seen it glamorized in teen media and decide to follow that example.

There is hope for this kind of groomer. Although they have learned an unhealthy pattern of behavior, it is possible for them to learn new, healthier ways of relating. The difficulty lies in helping the groomer **want** to change. For many groomers, manipulating others has reaped pleasurable rewards, and therefore they are not highly motivated to change. Yet, change is still possible.

For a smaller percentage of groomers, grooming is caused by more serious and difficult life issues. This type of groomer is tuned in only to his own needs and desires, and is extremely confused about the true nature of friendship, sex, and love. Some may live in families where there is little love and care but lots of problems. They may have been severely rejected by parents or loved ones, and often they've been abused themselves. They may have suffered the pain of being used and are now using others. Most of these groomers have little or no knowledge of normal emotional, physical, or sexual boundaries. This type of groomer is most likely acting out of deep-seated hurt and pain and will need professional help to change. If you encounter teens with these kinds of issues, please refer them to a professional who can help.

Regardless of why groomers do what they do, the end result is that they hurt someone else. We need to dissuade groomers from grooming, and enable teens to recognize and avoid the hurt caused by falling for a sexual con game.

The Emotional Grooming Process

There are two key elements that the emotional groomer must have in place in order to successfully control someone else — a false sense of trust and secrecy.

False sense of trust – The first stage of emotional grooming is developing a false sense of trust. A groomer convinces his target that he is the only person in the world who can really be trusted. The groomer swears that his life revolves around the target: *"You're all I think about." "You're my*

everything." "You're the only one who really understands me." At the same time, the groomer also tries to convince his target that he is (or should be) the most important person in her life: *"I'll always be there for you." "No one could love you the way I do." "I'll always protect you."*

The groomer also attempts to build trust by saying over and over that this relationship is good and natural: *"Everything is all right." "Don't worry, I'll take care of you."* The groomer usually does take care of his targets; he may buy them gifts, or protect them from others, or treat them with favoritism. The groomer skillfully connects much of what he does with the word "love:" *"This is the way it's meant to be. This is what real 'love' is all about."* The target is easy prey once she feels sure that the groomer is loyal and trusting, and is convinced of his "true" feelings.

Throughout this process, the target's loyalty is tested and the groomer's control is strengthened. After a groomer successfully weaves this web of false trust, his next step is to get the target to take part in some form of sexual behavior. The target is assured that having premarital sex not only is okay, but also is the "right" thing to do.

In healthy relationships, trust develops slowly and gradually. Trust is not earned by simply repeating over and over, *"Just trust me, baby!"* Trust is not based on the spoken word but on actions. It is through a person's behaviors, shown over time, that he or she proves worthy of trust.

The emotional groomer tries to rush this process and create a false sense of trust. The groomer is in a hurry to convince the target that he is dependable and trustworthy. The groomer will **talk** a lot about trust, especially telling the target why others should not be trusted, but allows no time for a real sense of trust to develop. In reality, the groomer is creating a false sense of trust. It certainly is not the trust that is present in healthy relationships. It is really an unhealthy dependence that is created by manipulation and deceit.

Teens who are hungry for attention and affection are prime targets for the emotional groomer. So are teens with poorly established boundaries. Such teens are eager to find someone they can trust, someone who will protect and befriend them. These teens don't have enough real life experience to recognize the characteristics of a trustworthy person. They are easy prey for the groomer's lines and sexual con games.

As mentioned earlier, this book contains excerpts from actual letters written by one teen to another. These letters illustrate how groomers go about developing a relationship with their targets. The following excerpts illustrate how the groomer tries to create a false sense of trust.

"I just want to talk to you in private with no one else around so I can tell you how I really feel. I won't do anything else, I promise. You will know that I can be trusted when you get to know me better. I would never hurt you or anything like that."

"No matter what happens to us I just want you to know if you need anybody to love or just talk to when you are down. I will always be available."

"I'll treat you right and I'm not going to do anything behind your back. You are what I live for. So without you my soul is black and my heart is empty. It might sound like I'm trying to get over on you but I'm not. I mean

everything I say. It comes from the heart. I cry almost every night hoping I could be with you. You're the best girl I ever had."

"We can't let anyone break us apart. If we get into an argument or disagreement we will work it out. People here can't be trusted. Only trust me."

What makes these lines believable? First of all, a sexual con artist will say these things over and over. She doesn't give up. She figures the more she says something, the more likely someone will fall for her game. She also will use other tactics designed to "prove" how trustworthy she is. It is extremely difficult for some unsuspecting teens to see through these words and actions to find the truth.

Secrecy – The second stage of emotional grooming is developing secrecy. Groomers persuade their targets to keep "our little secret" safe from others: *"No one, absolutely no one, can know about what we do."* This is one of the few times the groomer gives realistic reasons: *"I'll have to move away"* or *"We'll both get in trouble and not be able to see each other again."* The groomer does understand that he would be in trouble either legally or morally. For example, if the girl is a minor, he could go to jail; that's one of the reasons he works so hard to keep the relationship a secret. At the same time, however, he could be bragging to his friends about his "conquest" or how he "scored."

Another way the groomer develops secrecy is by telling the target that their relationship is different from anything anyone else has ever experienced: *"No one could possibly understand how deeply we love each other. We couldn't explain it. Why spoil everything by trying to tell them how we feel?"*

Sometimes, groomers use force or threats to make sure the target won't talk: *"If anyone finds out, you'll regret it for the rest of your life"* or *"You tell anyone and you're dead meat."* Other times, the threats involve other meaningful people in the target's life: *"You don't want your little sister to accidentally get hurt now, do you?"*

The groomer often does not have to carry through on any threats. Looks, stares, glares, or other body language can keep the target under his control. Once the target is afraid of what might happen if the secret is discovered, she will do almost anything to keep it hidden. The target is trapped. If anyone finds out, she believes she could be hurt or in trouble. She feels that the groomer holds all the power. If she wants to end the relationship and promises never to tell anyone, the groomer doesn't believe her. He continues to use whatever methods are necessary to keep the relationship a secret. Finally, the target feels that the situation is hopeless and that she's powerless to do anything about it. She begins believing that it's better to say nothing than to risk making everything worse, and she falls deeper and deeper into secrecy. The following excerpts illustrate how the groomer tries to keep the relationship from being discovered.

"We can still be secret lovers. And no one would have to know about it and it would just be our little secret. You know how much I care about you and hope you feel the same way."

"The main thing is that you just tell me about things and don't tell no one about us. I promise you that we will have some good times. Don't let the teachers see you writing letters. Write in private! Don't worry about getting scared off by all the rules. But don't say anything to anyone, it's our secret."

"I won't do you wrong. Just trust me and no one else. Don't be goin' to no one else cause they'll only do you wrong. This is just between you and me my love."

"The feelings we have for each other are true. And will stay that way. If we start going out, we can't let others get in our way. Just remember I really do care about you in many different ways and I've fallen in love with you. You're all I want. We have to be honest with each other. And we can't tell anyone about us. You know how fast stuff spreads around here. Let's just keep it to ourselves and no one will ever need to know."

Alcohol and Drugs

Before talking about other ways the sexual con artist manipulates, it's important to understand how alcohol and drugs affect both the target and the groomer. The groomer may use drugs or alcohol as an excuse: *"I didn't know what I was doing. I was so out of it"* or *"Don't blame me, I was drunk."* Drug and alcohol use also can make the sexual con artist even more aggressive and more likely to use force to get what he wants.

Drug and alcohol use often make the target easy prey for the groomer. Some teens end up involved in sexual behavior primarily because they were drunk or high. It's important to teach teens how drugs and alcohol affect the body. Drug or alcohol use can:

- Reduce inhibitions.

- Impair the ability to think clearly.

- Reduce or even totally impair the ability to make good decisions.

- Delay a person's response time.

- Cause a person to "black out" and be totally unaware of his or her situation.

Drug and alcohol use make it more likely that teens will make poor choices or let things go too far. Being under the influence reduces a person's ability to make good decisions and to recognize dangerous situations. Things that may seem harmless or fun when a person is drunk or high are real problems when the person sobers up.

Consider these statistics:

- Alcohol use by the victim, perpetrator or both has been implicated in 46 to 75 per cent of date rapes among college students.[1]

- One survey of college students found that 78 per cent of women had experienced sexual aggression (any type of sexual activity unwanted by the woman) while on a date. Dates on which sexual aggression occurred were more likely to include heavy drinking or drug use.[2]

- 55 per cent of teens say that having sex while drinking or on drugs is often a reason for unplanned teen pregnancies.[3]

- Among 18- to 22-year-old men and women, an earlier age at initiation of alcohol use is associated with the later likelihood of having multiple sex partners.[4]

Or consider these teens' experiences:[5]

"My very best friend had a guy take advantage of her when she was drunk and she got pregnant. She doesn't know who the father is to this day. She loves her son, but how is she going to explain what happened when he gets older?"

"A few of my friends have ended up sleeping with someone after drinking that they wouldn't have otherwise slept with. Drugs and alcohol make the choice easier because you don't think of the consequences."

"Alcohol has played probably the biggest role in my decisions about sex. Of the six people I have slept with, I was drunk with four of them."

"A friend of mine got really drunk at a party, slept with a guy she just met, and got AIDS. That one night of being intoxicated is going to cost her her life."

Language Cons

"Language cons" are the words and phrases – or "lines" – groomers use to trick and manipulate their targets. Language cons sometimes make a target feel special or desired; other times they make a target feel guilty or threatened. These lines may seem genuine or sincere when a target first hears them. Unfortunately, their real purpose is to control the target. Language cons are used to convince targets to do things they shouldn't do. Although these words may sound obvious or innocuous to adults, they can be very seductive to an unaware teenager. Ultimately, they also make targets feel powerless and helpless because they are repeated so often and are usually connected to some kind of consequence that the groomer controls. When youth hear things over and over, they are more likely to give in to what the groomer wants.

These lines are common language cons:

"It's okay. Don't worry."

"Just this once. Trust me."

"You know I wouldn't do anything to hurt you."

"This is normal. This is the way it's supposed to be."

"If you love me, prove it."

During the early stages of emotional grooming, the groomer uses language cons to gain the target's trust and develop secrecy. The language may seem harmless at first, but these lines help the groomer gain control. As the relationship progresses, the groomer will use more sexual phrases and will make vague references to sexual contact. The groomer may start out by using words that only hint about sex: *"If I had you alone, man, you wouldn't believe how good I could make you feel."*

If the groomer meets little or no resistance to subtle sexual language cons, the content of the language cons will become more sexually graphic and even offensive or obscene. The next step may be using slang words when talking about sexual body parts or behavior. Finally, the sexual act itself is graphically described – the perpetrator uses explicit, graphic, and vulgar language to determine whether the target is receptive to the grooming process. The groomer is "testing the water" – noting how much and what kind of sexual language the target will tolerate. If the target doesn't reject the groomer, the grooming continues. The language cons will lead into actual sexual contact. If the target does protest, the groomer will back off a little and try some other tactic. Many

times, however, the groomer doesn't give up and continues the harassment.

Language cons can seem very innocent or they may be terribly graphic. They may make a person feel good, or guilty, or threatened, or trusted. They may be sly or they may be overt. Most of the time, they are used to persuade a person into keeping a secret. They always are used to control another person.

Many groomers use the language of love to manipulate their targets. Groomers are aware that everyone wants to be loved, and so they do their best to convince their targets of undying love: *"I love you more each day. You're the greatest thing that ever happened to me. My love for you will last forever. I adore you."* Some targets are so hungry for love and attention that they easily fall for such lines. Most targets want to believe that someone could actually love and protect them, and they become blinded by all the attention they receive. Some targets may not have had a warm and caring home life and want someone to fill the emptiness they feel.

Targets may feel really confused by everything that is happening. At times, they may feel safe and cared for. Other times, they may be a little frightened and worried. Soon, a target finds that the relationship is frequently the only thing on her mind. Even though she may know the relationship has gone too far, she feels powerless or afraid to end it. The giving and receiving of attention become something she likes, even though there are other parts of the relationship she doesn't like.

Even though a target may realize that what the groomer wants is wrong, she may go ahead anyway. The target has been fooled into thinking that love and sex are the same, and that you can't have one without the other. If she wants to feel what she thinks is love – the groomer's attention and affection – then she must give sex. That is a distorted view of sexuality. Teenagers must know that the sexual act is not a "duty" nor an "obligation." And sex is no sign of loyalty and devotion to another person. Many targets also don't realize that an emotional groomer may have two or three other targets on the line at the same time. That certainly proves he isn't "loyal" or "devoted."

Aside from convincing a target to have sex, the groomer often talks him into doing other things that may result in trouble. Running away, drinking alcohol or using drugs, stealing, or getting revenge on someone are all things that groomers may convince their targets to do. The grooming process is usually the same – build a false sense of trust, and keep the relationship secret, then manipulate the person into doing something the groomer wants.

The more skilled and adept at emotional grooming the perpetrator is, the less he will rely on physical force. Emotional groomers rarely use physical force to coerce a person into a sexual act. This doesn't mean it hasn't happened. But usually, instead of using physical force to get sex, most groomers rely on the relationship they have established with their targets.

Most rape targets experience a trauma that is different from what targets of emotional grooming feel. Women and men who have been forced in painful, violent ways to have sex against their will, see themselves as victims and readily recognize the criminal aspect of rape. These victims know they were not "willing participants" during their abuse.

While many targets of emotional grooming may feel humiliated or embarrassed when they realize they have been used, they often are not aware of the criminal aspects of the grooming relationship. These targets have been convinced that they are willing participants; they may even have been convinced that they "caused" the relationship. A groomer can twist the truth to make the target think that the groomer is innocent, that nothing is wrong with the relationship, or that anything that happens is the target's fault. The truth is that the emotional groomer is a criminal, a con artist who is just devious and shrewd enough to get away with the crime.

Emotional grooming is a process of manipulation and control. The words a groomer uses are carefully chosen. A groomer says what the target most needs to hear to get her to do what he wants. The language of a groomer is a con, a trick, a game. The language cons of a groomer are not just "pick-up lines." They are part of a larger plan for using another person.

Characteristics of Language Cons

The following characteristics are evident in the language of emotional groomers and players; these are the elements that set their language apart from the norm. Encourage teens to use this list to analyze the language of a potential groomer.

■ **Trying to convince the target that sex and love are the same thing** – that having sex is the only way to prove love

■ **Specific, graphic, and even offensive sexual references**

- **Coercive** – using words that threaten or intimidate

- **Possessive** – treating and talking about the target like an object that is owned

- **Repetitive** – constantly using the same words to gain the target's trust

- **Referring to sexual behavior as a "duty" or "responsibility"**

- **Referring to sexual behavior as the ultimate proof of loyalty or maturity**

- **Controlling** – using words that reinforce the groomer's position as "the boss"

Even when a target tries to end the relationship, the groomer will continue to use language cons. He certainly isn't going to take the blame or admit that any type of harmful relationship ever existed. He definitely isn't going to confess that he did anything wrong. He may lie, make threats, or try to convince others that the target is crazy. Sometimes, the groomer will say that the target made everything up: *"She's always wanted me, but since I didn't pay any attention to her, she just says things to get back at me."*

It can be very difficult for a target to find the best way to stop the abuse. When targets feel powerless and afraid, they are at a loss for what to do. Some targets don't make good choices; they try to solve the problem by running away, hurting themselves, getting further involved with alcohol and drugs, or even attempting suicide. Targets who tell someone who can help, like a trusted adult or older friend, stand the best chance of getting out of the abusive situation. Many

targets turn to teachers or counselors for advice.

Many groomers blame their targets for everything that happened: *"It was all your fault. You're nothing but a whore! If you hadn't wanted me so much, none of this would have ever happened."* This type of verbal abuse just adds to the guilt, shame, and hopelessness that the target may already feel.

The target should realize that the groomer will be just as manipulative trying to get out of the relationship as he was getting into it. Sometimes, other people won't believe what the target says at first. This is partly because the groomer used language cons with them, too. Through manipulation, he has persuaded other people to believe him. However, if the target has the courage to tell the truth, and not give up, she is on the road to recovery.

Responding to Language Cons

Some people call language cons "lines." "Lines" or language cons are thinly veiled come-on statements or outright lies used to seduce or coerce someone into sexual activity. To remember what a **line** really is, just remove the "n"- and see the **lie**.

When responding to language cons it's important for teens to:

- Understand that language cons are used to trick, manipulate, and deceive. People who use language cons are selfish and untrustworthy.

- Learn how to recognize language cons. Pay close attention to a person's behaviors as well as his or her words. The old saying, "A picture is worth a thousand words," applies here. Observe how a person treats others, and listen to what he or she says to others about dating, relationships, and sex. All of these can be important indicators of an emotional groomer's hidden intentions.

- Learn and practice good social skills. Developing good communication and refusal skills can help in resisting threats or coercion. Build strong relationships with trustworthy adults you can go to for advice.

- Not waste time blaming themselves. Sexual con artists need to bear the responsibility for their words and actions. If you become a target, focus on doing things to get better rather than blaming yourself.

- Understand that there are no excuses for using another person, especially in sexual ways. People who use language cons really only want to please themselves, not others.

- Realize that the person who uses language cons will most likely be quite persistent and use many different angles. You have to be just as persistent and not give in.

- Create and maintain healthy same-gender friendships. Find good friends of the same gender who have your best interests at heart. These kinds of friends can "watch your back" and help you hear and see what you may not want to notice about someone else. In other words, friends can help each other unmask a sexual con artist.

What to Say

Saying "no" to someone is difficult, especially if that person is skilled at using language cons. Some people are so "smooth" with words that teens may not be able to figure out their real intentions. Therefore, it's always wise to stop and think before agreeing to do something that may result in negative consequences.

Sexual con artists will use various kinds of lines ranging from "sweet talk" and flattery, to sexual innuendo and outright graphic sexual language. The groomer will use whatever kind of language con it takes to get what he or she wants. Sexual con artists can be very persuasive. And, convincing someone to have sex tops their list of priorities.

Having some idea of how to respond can help teens avoid the verbal traps set by someone who wants to convince another to have sex. Teens can use one of the following statements to help stay in control when responding to a line.

"You don't really want me; you want sex."

"I'm not ready for sex. Don't try to push me into doing it."

"If you really care for me, you'll understand."

"Love is not sex; love is a commitment to make each other better."

"Real love isn't over in just a few minutes."

"You don't own my body. And I'm certainly not renting it out."

"Love is a two-way street. You only want it one way: your way."

"I respect myself. Why can't you?"

"My brain's between my ears, not my legs."

"I want you to love me, not my body."

"I want real love, not an imitation."

"I have too much to lose."

"It's not worth it."

"Love is based on friendship, and you don't hurt friends."

"I want to be respected, not dejected."

"What part of 'no' don't you understand?"

"I know you don't understand, but I want you to respect my feelings."

"I care enough about you to do what's best for both of us."

"It's not right. I hope you understand."

"When I said 'No,' I meant it."

Saying 'No'

This letter was written by a 16-year-old girl to a 14-year-old boy who had frequently written her notes that he gave her at band practice. Notice the various ways in which she said "no."

"Hello. I am going to be very blunt and honest with you. NO. I do not like you at all and I have no interest in getting to know you whatsoever. First of all, you are younger than me and I am looking for different qualities in a guy than what you have. No, there's nothing wrong with you but I want someone different and maturity is a main quality. Please quit writing me notes. No, I'm not going to give you a chance. Yes, you are wasting your time. Sorry, but I'm a blunt person. Lay off.

[1] The Centers for Disease Control and Prevention, Youth Risk Behavior Surveillance -United States, 1999, Morbidity and Mortality Weekly Report, June 2000, vol. 49.

[2] Ibid.

[3] The National Center of Addiction and Substance Abuse (CASA) at Columbia University, Dangerous Liaisons: Substance Abuse and Sex, New York, 1999.

[4] Santelli, J.S., et al., Timing of alcohol and other drug use and sexual risk behaviors among unmarried adolescents and young adults, Family Planning Perspectives, 2001, vol. 33.

[5] Quotes are from National Campaign to Prevent Teen Pregnancy, *Weekly Teen Survey: Sex Has Consequences*, April 18-28, 2000.

The Nine Grooming Tactics

2

So how do we help teens learn how to recognize a groomer? Learning what emotional grooming is, the elements of the grooming process, and the language cons used by groomers are all helpful tools

teens can learn to help them better recognize a sexual con artist. Groomers can also be identified by the specific tactics they use to manipulate others. Once teens can recognize these nine grooming tactics as manipulative and unhealthy behaviors, they can more easily detect and avoid the "players." The nine tactics are:

- Jealousy and possessiveness

- Insecurity

- Intimidation

- Anger

- Accusations

- Flattery

- Status

- Bribery

- Control

Please note that some of these tactics, outside of an emotional grooming relationship, are normal feelings. These normal feelings only become grooming tactics when that feeling is used to manipulate someone else. Then it becomes a harmful and wrong use of that emotion. Jealousy, insecurity, and anger are all normal human emotions, but when used to manipulate or control someone else, they become grooming tactics.

Take jealousy, for example. Even though it's not a happy feeling, it is common and most people have felt jealous at one time or another. Imagine that a teen sees her boyfriend standing very close to and talking with a very attractive girl. Perhaps the teen feels jealous. That would be normal. However, it is how she acts on that jealousy that makes her reaction harmful or healthy. If she beats up the other woman, threatens to hurt herself, or damages her boyfriend's car, she is acting in a way that is meant to manipulate her boyfriend into paying full attention to her. That's emotional grooming.

So how can teens handle feeling jealous (or angry or insecure) without resorting to grooming? The teen in the example above should recognize and own that she's feeling jealous, and then tell her boyfriend or a trusted adult how she feels. Together they can find a constructive way to deal with the situation and then let it go. That's a healthy response to the difficult feeling of jealousy.

Most of the nine grooming tactics are **always** manipulative and **always** unhealthy in any relationship. Take, for example, the grooming tactics of bribery and intimidation. No matter what, intimidation and bribery should never happen in a healthy relationship. Never. Teach teens not to tolerate such behavior. Encourage teens to discontinue hanging around with or dating someone who threatens, intimidates or tries to bribe them. Nothing good will come of a relationship like that.

Following are descriptions of the nine grooming tactics and excerpts from notes and letters written by and to teens. Each excerpt illustrates one or more of the tactics groomers use to manipulate and control others.

Jealousy and Possessiveness

As mentioned before, jealousy is a normal, albeit difficult, human emotion. Jealousy only becomes a grooming tactic when it is used to control or manipulate someone else. Acting out in a jealous rage, spreading vicious rumors, attempting to emotionally or physically hurt someone you are jealous of, or using jealousy to manipulate someone – these are examples of emotional grooming.

A groomer may express his jealousy through possessive and controlling words and behaviors. The groomer doesn't want anyone else "messing" with his "territory." This may include attempting to control whom the target can talk to or hang out with, how she can dress, or even how she spends money. The groomer acts as if he completely owns his target's feelings and behaviors and is resentful and extremely jealous of anyone who gets any kind of attention from his "possession."

"I'm telling you now and one time only, I want his stuff out of your locker. What kind of fool do I look like? I'm going out with you, but your ex-boyfriend is still in your locker. No! That is not going to happen. I want his stuff out. Today! If you're my girl his stuff has to go."

Treating someone like an object to own rather than a person to relate to is at the heart of jealousy and possessiveness. Teens may see and hear signs of this everywhere: *"She's my woman." "You can't talk to her." "You belong to me,"* and so on. They need to be reminded that people are not objects to be owned or possessed or controlled, but are persons to relate to.

There's another way a groomer might use jealousy to control her target. She may attempt to make the target feel jealous in order to get him to "prove" his love. She may say or do things to provoke feelings of jealousy and possessiveness.

"I want us to be together for the rest of our days, but I do need some type of "social" life with boys cuz baby you ain't giving none up."

Using jealousy to control or "own" someone else or trying to provoke feelings of jealousy in someone else are both grooming tactics. Both are signs that a relationship is off to an unhealthy start.

But everyone feels jealous some time or another, right? True! But the key to having healthy relationships lies in learning how to handle jealousy, and all our other feelings, appropriately. One method teens can use to handle emotions appropriately is to **Name, Claim** and **Tame** their feelings. Here is how to describe this method to teens:

NAME – Spend some time figuring out what it is you are feeling. Often we just react to negative or difficult feelings without really being aware of the actual emotion. It is helpful to name your feeling, so that you can move beyond it.

CLAIM – To claim your feeling means to "own" it. *"I feel jealous"* is different than *"You make me so jealous."* Using "I" language helps us to recognize the feeling as our own, rather than blaming it on others.

TAME – Taming a feeling means finding a way to express it appropriately, without hurting yourself or someone else. Usually this means finding a trusted adult or wise friend who will enable you to name and claim your feelings, encourage you to find ways to express feelings appropriately, (like journaling, talking it out, crying, counseling, etc.), and finally who will support you in accepting and letting go of the emotion. Taming ultimately involves recognizing and accepting what you can and cannot control

in life. It's not an easy process, but it will help you to grow and to have happier and healthier relationships.

Insecurity

Like jealousy, insecurity is a normal human emotion. In some cases, it's even appropriate to feel somewhat insecure. And like jealousy, insecurity is a grooming tactic **only** when it is used to manipulate someone else.

The groomer uses insecurity to manipulate in two ways. One way the groomer misuses insecurity is to act insecure and ask for constant reassurance of the target's love and loyalty. The target is expected to take care of this insecurity by writing love letters or telling the groomer how great she is and how much she is loved. She also may want pity and sympathy – someone to feel sorry for her.

"I guess it's no big deal. I just don't think I'm really your type or good enough for you. I'm screwing too many things up. I'm not worth it. So let me know if you want to stop our relationship, I'll try to understand. I probably deserve it anyway. The way I treat you, I'm not doing it the way I'm supposed to. I guess I was wrong. I'm sorry for treating you the way I did."

The groomer may take insecurity so far as to say something like *"I'll kill myself if you leave me!"* Teens should use great caution if they hear this statement. It may just be an idle threat, a ploy used to get the target to stay in the relationship. But we never know for sure what someone else's true intentions are. When teens hear of anyone threatening to hurt themselves or someone else, they should tell an adult – a parent, a teacher, a counselor, a police officer, or a pastor.

It is never a teen's obligation to stay in a relationship with someone who is threatening self-harm or to hurt others, but it is an obligation to tell an adult who can help. Threats of self-harm can sometimes turn into harm acted out toward others. Criminal justice advocate, Laura Delgado, says it this way, "A threat of suicide is exactly the same as a threat of homicide. It says that 'I don't have anything to lose.'"

The other misuse of insecurity is when the groomer attempts to magnify the target's insecurities or create new insecurities.

"No one else will ever want you. I'm the only one who is ever going to want you. You'd be stupid to pass up a guy like me. I'm the man. Once I'm through with you, you'll never want anybody else."

This kind of manipulation is an attempt to control the target's thoughts and feelings about herself. The groomer hopes that the target will feel so bad and so insecure about herself that she will stay in a relationship with the groomer and become more reluctant to open up to others.

Intimidation

Intimidation is a powerful form of manipulation. Unlike jealousy or insecurity, intimidation is not a normal human emotion and has no place in healthy relationships.

The groomer intimidates by frightening, coercing, or threatening others into submission. The intimidation can be verbal, nonverbal, or a combination of both. Some groomers are quite skilled at intimidating

and getting what they want from others with just a glance or a gesture. Intimidation is always wrong and is always manipulative.

One type of verbal intimidation is threatening. For example, a groomer may threaten to hurt the target or someone close to the target, threaten to take a favorite possession of the target and damage or destroy it as a warning of what could happen, or threaten to "tell" something the target has done wrong.

Verbal intimidation is used to make the target feel uncomfortable and uneasy and the groomer to feel in control. Groomers use intimidating and threatening language to "test the waters" and see how much a target will tolerate. These verbal scare tactics usually work; the target becomes too afraid to say "no" and may even worry about his or her safety.

"I'm not mad at you, as long as you're not lying to me. If I find out you are lying, you and me are finished. So, if you're not telling me something, you better spill it now. I don't want to have to find out later from someone else. I can find out!"

"I'm sure I confused the s--- out of you. One minute I'm mean to you, the next minute I'm whispering I love you while tapping your chest with my water bottle. It was all a play for the girls."

Another form of verbal intimidation is when the groomer uses sexually explicit and/ or offensive language when speaking to the target. The groomer may:

- Use vulgar sexual language in front of the target.

- Make sexual noises or sounds (cat calls, howling, barking, etc.).

- Use specific, graphic sexual descriptions of what the groomer wants to do to the target.

- Ask questions that are too personal or too sexual in nature.

The groomer uses graphic or offensive sexual language for various reasons:

- To scare the target into participating in the described sexual behavior

- To desensitize the target so that he or she will become used to this kind of language and eventually this kind of sexual behavior

- To test the target's limits and boundaries – if the target laughs, giggles, or even just ignores sexually explicit or obscene language, it gives the groomer the "green light" to continue

- To push for sexual activity

- To sexually arouse the target

Teens do not have to tolerate, listen to, or participate in sexually explicit, obscene, or offensive language. It's best for teens to just walk away from language like this. Better yet, if this kind of talk is taking place at school functions, in notes, e-mails, or pictures, teens should be encouraged to tell a teacher or administrator. Often this kind of language can be a form of sexual harassment – and sexual harassment is illegal!

Often the groomer will use threatening words in conjunction with intimidating physical actions – looming over someone who is seated, standing too close, touching or grabbing others, using loud and controlling voice tones and language, staring at sexual body parts, hitting the palm of the hand very hard, snapping a pencil in two, or faking a punch. Male groomers may take intimidating stances when girls walk by – slouching over, holding their hands on their crotches, howling, whistling, or making cat calls. These sexually graphic, offensive, or vulgar gestures can also be forms of sexual harassment. Students should not tolerate it. They should report it!

Anger

Like jealousy, anger is a normal human emotion. In some circumstances, anger can even be justifiable and produce positive change. But none of this is true when a groomer uses anger to manipulate.

For the groomer, angry outbursts are a way to control and get what they want from others. Unfortunately, using explosive anger to get what you want is depicted and often glorified in many types of contemporary media – from TV talk shows to music videos. And all too often adults do not model appropriate ways of expressing and managing angry feelings. The result is that many teens lack the modeling and social skills necessary for proper anger management.

More and more teens are misusing anger in dating relationships or allowing themselves to get hurt by others' uncontrolled anger. Teen dating violence is on the rise. Consider these statistics:

- One in every five high school girls has been physically or sexually abused by a dating partner.[1]

- A disturbing number of boys have adopted attitudes that men are entitled to control their girlfriends through violence.[2]

■ A 1999 survey of Massachusetts students reported that 16 per cent of girls and 6 per cent of boys have had sexual contact against their will.[3]

A groomer's anger can be displayed in a variety of ways – yelling, screaming, hitting, or throwing things. Regardless of how it is expressed, the groomer's explosive anger is used to threaten, intimidate, and manipulate others. And whenever anger is used to manipulate and hurt others, it's wrong.

Because he usually gets what he wants from others when he misuses his anger in this way, the groomer will use angry out-bursts to threaten or intimidate his target into some kind of sexual act. Since the target doesn't want to lose her boyfriend or may be afraid that he will take his anger out on her, she engages in the sexual behavior.

> *"I've told you not to mess with me! People get hurt when they mess with me. Unless I find out your lying to me. If I find out you are, be ready, because I'm going off. That's why I said if you left something out, tell me now."*

An emotional groomer who uses anger to manipulate and intimidate others can be very dangerous. His outbursts may happen more frequently or become more violent. He may even connect sex with the power his angry outbursts have given him. After a while, he may believe that sex is good only when force or pain is involved.

> *"Today I seen JJ when I was outside with everyone. He came up there and snatched me up then beat my ass. I fought back, I don't give a f--- who he is. Then after awhile, my stomach started hurting and I threw up. Later I was laying on his lap and he said he was sorry and we ended up doin' the nasty."*

Even some of the language used to describe the sex act is violent. Some groomers describe sex with phrases like "knocking boots," "Let's hit it," "I'm gonna get me a piece of that," "Tag that a--," or "thumping." Words like "tag," "hit," "knock," or "thump" reveal the groomer's true intent – to hurt and use another person. Referring to the other person as an object – "piece of that," "it," or "bones" – enables the groomer to distance himself from the target and makes it easier to use another person.

Some forms of contemporary media, especially music and music videos, con-tribute to this connection between sex and violence. Spend some time listening to or reading lyrics of various contemporary songs and you will find violent references to sexu-al activity. The numerous repetitions of such violent sexual imagery only serves to make it seem more "normal" or acceptable and ends up desensitizing some teens and adults to its aggressive and unhealthy nature.

Herein lies the problem: if teens think and talk about sex in violent and aggressive terms (and we know many teens and adults do use violent terminology when "joking" around or singing along with favorite songs), then it follows that sooner or later they will act on sex in this manner – being violent or aggressive in a sexual relationship or allow-ing someone to mistreat them in this way. It's like a "chain reaction;" the way we talk about something influences the way we think about something, and that in turn will influence the way we behave. The following poem offers good advice when it comes to the connection between thoughts, words, and behaviors.

Chain Reaction

Examine and screen your thoughts

Because your thoughts become
    your words

Your words become your actions

Your actions become your habits

Your habits become your character

And your character becomes
    your destiny

                    – Anonymous

Accusations

When using this tactic, the groomer creates false or exaggerated accusations to frighten, threaten and ultimately control the target. For example, a groomer might accuse his girlfriend of doing all sorts of things that she didn't do. He might accuse her of having sex with other guys or talking about him behind his back. Regardless of the specifics of the accusation, the real intent is to publicly intimidate and perhaps even humiliate the target, thus maximizing the groomer's sense of control.

> *"Just tell me or not if you did anything with Booker. If you want him, just go out with him. I'll get over it. It's not like you would really care anyway. He even came up to me and said some things about you and him, and what you did. Don't do this to me, even when I hear this stuff, it hurts my feelings. I wouldn't be surprised if you're playing on me."*

Flattery

Most emotional groomers are "smooth talkers." They know what to say and how to say it so that they impress others and appear completely trustworthy. They use language cons that lure the target into thinking she is the most important person in his world, and that he's the best guy for her. The groomer does not give sincere or honest compliments. He merely uses flattery – exaggerated and insincere comments – to get what he wants. Sometimes, the flattery may be appropriate, but it usually is sexually suggestive or graphic. Even though the groomer's flattery may be insincere and manipulative, the target may still enjoy the attention.

> *"I wanted to say 'I like you' when I first saw you. You made me feel special. Lucky is the guy who gets to be with a diamond like you, your eyes are so beautiful your body your hair, everything. You are like candy, once a guy gets a taste of you he will go crazy. And one day he won't taste it, he'll eat it."*

> *"I know a lot of guys like me, but I don't like them. You seem like a nice person to me. I hope that one day you and I will be closer together. You look good and you know it."*

We all like to hear nice things said about us. But it's important to know the difference between flattery and sincere compliments. With flattery there's always a string attached, something wanted or expected in return. Compliments are different. Compliments are given to make the other person feel good. No strings are attached.

A sincere and genuine compliment shows approval or admiration for people or for their accomplishments. It is specific and truthful. Learning how to give and how to accept compliments are important relationship-building skills for teens. When complimenting others, rather than focusing on a person's looks, they should try paying attention to and complimenting others for what they have accomplished or who they are on the inside, their personal qualities. Giving sincere compliments that recognize a person's talents and accomplishments is a sure way to make someone's day and to get a relationship started in the right direction.

Status

Sometimes, others "look up to" the groomer. He could be a good athlete; she might have a lot of money; he may have access to alcohol or drugs, or she may be the most popular or most attractive girl in school. Whatever the reason for the status, the groomer uses his or her popularity to lure a target into a sexual relationship. More often than not, the target likes hanging around with someone with so much status and popularity and will often be convinced that sex is "owed" to the emotional groomer because of the attention, popularity, or favors the groomer's status gives the target.

> *"I do like you a lot even though we're not going out. If I didn't would I waste 5 minutes of a phone call on you? Would I call you when there's a lot more girls that I could be calling or would I even talk to you? I'm not too good for you at all because there's no such thing. Please believe me I do care and like you and I wouldn't be wasting my time if I didn't."*

> *"I understand that you want a fine babe like me, so don't get all choked up. You treat me right and you'll see what that brings you."*

For some, having sex also can be a way to gain status. Some teens think having sex will prove they are "macho," "cool" or "grown up." These teens are easy prey for the emotional groomer.

Bribery

Bribery is "giving to get." The groomer may give material things to his target, but these "gifts" always have a string attached. In healthy relationships, giving gifts can be a normal sign of friendship or love. In an unhealthy relationship, a groomer gives "gifts" in order to bribe or manipulate the target. The target may think that something, usually some sort of sexual behavior, must be done to "pay back" the groomer so that the attention and gifts will continue.

Sometimes, the bribe that convinces a target to stay with a groomer may be the promise of marriage or of always being together. Female groomers will often use the promise of sex as a bribe to get and keep a guy in a relationship. In some relationships, the bribes are alcohol or drugs. This is an old trick used by pimps with their prostitutes: Get them addicted to a substance and they will give you everything you want in exchange for more of the drug.

> *"If I could do it I'd buy you everything you wanted. Remember that sweater at the mall. That would look so good on you baby. Someday I'll buy it or steal it if I have to. You mean the world to me and I want to show you how much. You just keep being good to me, you'll see."*

Bribery can sometimes be very blatant and very destructive. A 16-year-old girl told this story to her teacher: *"When I was 13, my boyfriend, who was 19, took me to the fair. He won one of those big stuffed teddy bears. When we got home he told me he'd give me the bear if I had sex with him. How come when he was on top of me, I started crying?"* The teacher responded, *"You cried because he was taking something* precious from you that you weren't ready to give. That's where the tears came from." It's obvious that this groomer used bribery to get what he wanted. He gave a 13-year-old girl a toy in order to get sex from her.

Unfortunately, this attitude of "giving to get" appears to be widespread among many boys and men in our society. In a recent survey, 30 per cent of seventh to ninth grade boys believed that a girl owes them sex if they spend a lot of money on her. Even more frightening is the attitude that it is acceptable to force sex on a girl if necessary. This type of thinking is devastating to the moral, sexual, and social development of young people.

Control

The ultimate goal of an emotional groomer is to gain control of the target and of the relationship. The groomer wants to control not only what his target does, but also how he or she thinks and feels. The groomer seeks to gain power or dominance in the relationship by using any or all of the grooming tactics described. Remember, some groomers are "playing" this game of control and manipulation with two or three other targets at the same time. If a particular tactic won't work with one target, the groomer will try it with another target.

"If you get in trouble doing anything wrong and I hear about it, you will deal with me. I don't want to do anything with any other girl except you. I'm the only one who is right for you. So don't play on me, OK. You wouldn't want to see me mad. Just do what I say. If you're smart you'll listen good."

"I really do love you baby and I don't want you to feel like your being pressured into this relationship. But you gotta know that I'm the man. I want you to be positive about this relationship I don't want you to have the impression that if you see me talking to another girl that I'm playing you. I want to be true and I want you to think I'm being true to this relationship. Yo baby I want this relationship to work out. I won't do you wrong. Just trust me."

These are signs that someone is too controlling. He or she:

- Constantly calls to check up on you.

- Tells you how to dress, who to hang out with, how to spend your time or money.

- Forces or manipulates others into doing what he or she wants.

- Sends harassing or threatening e-mails, messages, or notes.

- Abuses others physically, emotionally, or sexually.

- Uses violence or intimidation to get his or her way.

- Humiliates or puts you down in public.

- Make demands or gives orders.

- Tries to get you to keep the relationship a secret.

- Has an explosive temper – throws objects, slams doors, punches walls, etc.

- Refuses to listen to or show respect to others.

- Attempts to keep you away from friends or family.

- Gives gifts to get something in return.
- Spreads rumors about you.
- Threatens suicide or self-harm.

The Results of Being Groomed

The following is a letter written by a young woman expressing how she feels after realizing she's been groomed:

"How ya doing? I'm doing ok, but not the best. I have some things I kinda need to get off my chest and I need to do it now! OK! You were a great friend before everything happened. I loved being around you and enjoyed you as a person! I always had a crush on you and always wanted us to become closer. Then you started talking to Keisha more. And I had class with you so that gave me the chance to get to know you and I jumped on it! I felt very good about how our relationship was going. But something inside wanted to get to know you better! I don't know how to say it. Then there was that night! That night I enjoyed very much! I haven't had those feelings in a long time! But, those feelings got mixed up somewhere. I knew nothen was gonna happen with us. So, I wasn't waiting for you to come up and ask me out! But, well, I don't know what I expected. OK, I'm going to put this as clear as I can! What I did that night was something special. I don't do that with just any guy. I felt that everything was ok. But then when I got back and the first thing I hear about is me and you did what, I felt nasty! I heard what you said I did and I didn't know what to do. I felt like a pile of s- – -. I guess I felt used in a way. My two weeks have been hell!! I couldn't hold

anything down, I got depressed all the time, I was scared to go to school, and I feel like I lost a great friend because of all this! Sometimes I wish none of this ever happened to me. I have been hurt by too many guys. I don't feel right around you! I feel like I was used for a free night and then forgot about. Left in the dust for the next person to come along. I feel sick! I can't even face you as myself anymore because I feel so bad!"

Obviously, her words speak volumes of the hurt caused by grooming. If you analyze her letter closely, you'll notice the groomer used various tactics to manipulate her into a sexual encounter. He successfully developed a false sense of trust, then used jealousy and insecurity by making sure that she noticed him talking to and spending time with other girls. For this young woman, and many other guys and girls like her, the results of grooming are emotionally devastating.

The following letters are examples of how language cons and grooming tactics were used in another relationship. The first four letters were written by an 18-year-old boy to a 12-year-old girl. He used many of the manipulative methods discussed in this chapter. He said they were going to take it slow. He told her how special she was and how he would always be there for her. He was telling her, sometimes subtly and sometimes overtly, that she should trust him and that he would take care of her. And he told her what she wanted to hear, again and again. Unfortunately, she believed him.

"Hi honey. How are you. When I said I would give you something special, I take that back. I don't want you to think anything about that. I want you to do good cause hopefully you'd feel good and that would make me feel good.

Speaking of good asses, you got a nice one yourself. I like you for what you are not what you can give. It's just that sometimes when I'm around you I feel like doing this and that. I want to get closer and stuff and don't do all this negative stuff. Then nature can take its time. Let's get closer but don't go too far. I want you badly. But I will wait if I have to. I have other stuff to say but I don't want to write it down."

"What's up my love? I have been thinking about you night and day. I've been thinking about how much I love you which is a lot. Some other things I've been thinking about is when I first saw you and when I held you in my arms in back of the school. I miss you so much. I can't wait to see you again. There's a lot of things I love about you. You're smart, you have a sweet personality and you are very pretty. You are very special to me. Just thinking about you makes me happy. I really want to be there for you. You are too sweet to be taken advantage of and treated bad. And I don't want that to happen. I do like to do it, but, we are going to take it nice and slow. You know what I'm saying. Some time I will show you how much I love you, but not right now. Gotta go."

"What's Up? How are you doin' sweetheart? Myself, thinking about you mostly. I wish I could be with you so much. I called you back last night and your mom answered the phone and she told me that I couldn't call you anymore because I was too old to talk to you. I know you don't like that any more than I do but I promise you we will work around that. Because I like you too much and no matter what anybody says, I will always be there for you. Nobody can keep us apart. I want you to be my girl. I want to ask you face to face so

you can see for yourself how serious I am. I love you and I want you to be happy. You deserve a lot of tender lovin' care, and I want to be the one to give it to you. That's from the bottom of my heart."

"How are you doin'? Myself, I'm takin' it E.Z. I had a lovely time with you yesterday. You really lightened my day. I want you to know that I think you are a very attractive and sweet person. But, I am a lot older than you and where I come from they call it "robbin' the cradle." You know what I'm saying. Even tho' age is just a number. I still like you and want to get to know you real good. If you know what I mean. I don't want any of these players here trying to take advantage of you because you're young. I want to be there for you. If anybody gets you, it better be me. You're so special to me. Write back. "

This letter was written by the girl:

"Hi. How are you? Did you have fun with me last night? Yes or no. I had fun, but I wondered how you liked it? I will always love you baby. My mom found out about us. Now, I can't call boys and they can't call me. But, I will call you, OK? I will find a way. You are the only one who I love. I know I can trust you totally. And, I hope you had fun with me last night. I had never done that before. I hoped you liked it. You are nice and loveable and I think about you every day. I hope you will be there for me. I will give you anything you want and in a big way. If I can't have you I don't know what I'll do. I feel like killing myself right now. And I do hope I kill myself and sorry I said that."

It is evident that the boy had control of this girl. She needed him because he was bigger and older, and she trusted him. She was convinced that he offered her emotional security and protection. This girl had been emotionally and sexually abused as a young child. She thought she had to have sex with someone to be loved. In reality, she was being skillfully manipulated again.

Most examples of language cons presented so far have contained subtle sexual messages. Many have mentioned or centered on love, emotional security, trust, and secrecy. The letter from the following youth is very direct and graphic. Aside from the braggadocio in the letter, it is obvious that this youth is unable to differentiate sexual behavior from affection. Although we may be shocked and disgusted at what the youth says, we have to be aware that some youth talk and think like this. Youth with poor emotional and physical boundaries may even find this language attractive or arousing. It is difficult to teach youth the emotional and responsible side to an affectionate, caring relationship when the sexual act is all they have ever equated to love.

"I heard that you are mad when I don't kiss you. The reason why is because I don't want to get you in trouble. So I want to but we can't be out in the open. If you want sex, I give it to you anytime, anywhere. You're not strange about thinking about that, you should keep thinking about that. When I get done with you, I don't know if you would be able to think straight. I also heard you said you had a small gap, I wish I knew that. If it is small I make that m---f--- bigger, I make your nipples sore too. I would take care of you in all ways. You got a nice ass too. I like it just right. Another reason why sometimes I won't tell you I love you is because if I did you might think one day if I did something wrong to you,

you might think I don't love you. That I was just saying that. That is wrong, I need you baby. But if you are serious about getting f---d, just let me know."

This letter is a reflection of the type of graphic and explicit sexual language used by many of today's teens. The above letter was written by a young man. But young men are not the only ones using sexually explicit language to groom and manipulate others. Some teen girls are using similar language to arouse and control young men.

"Boo – I'm sitting in class thinking of you. Tonight will be fun. I'm not sure what I'm going to wear. I'm thinking about <u>nothing</u>, but you might like that <u>too</u> much! But, I can wear a skirt for easy access! We might be able to work something out on the bus tonight!!"

More and more teens, and even some adults, consider this kind of sexually explicit language normal because they hear it on television, in music, in movies, and tragically, often in their homes. Unfortunately, many people in our society have become desensitized and are less aware of how dangerous, violent, and degrading such language is.

[1] Journal of American Medical Association, August 2001.

[2] Ibid.

[3] Massachusetts Dept. of Ed., 1999, www.doe.mass.edu.

How the Media Groom Youth

Emotional grooming is not limited to human relationships. Media messages are grooming many teens and some adults. Remember grooming is nothing more than a con game. The goal of a con game is to manipulate, persuade, or coerce someone into doing what the groomer wants. The sexual imagery and content in media and advertising are used to persuade consumers to buy certain products or make lifestyle choices.

Examples of Media Grooming

Many advertisers and media moguls admit that they'll do whatever it takes to get and keep your attention and your brand loyalty. Take, for example, a catalog produced by the popular pre-teen and teen clothier, Abercrombie and Fitch.

■ The 1999 holiday "Naughty and Nice" issue included nudity, descriptions of sexuality, and an interview with a porn star.

■ Another Christmas edition included a picture of four girls in bed with a young man holding up his boxers.

■ Other issues have included photos of a nude female, breasts exposed, embraced from behind by a naked man, and a lesbian couple kissing at their "wedding."[1]

A high-ranking Abercrombie and Fitch executive commented to The New York Times, "I pay so little attention to the critics who feel youth ought to be locked in boxes until they're 50. All I care about is the target audience and how that person is feeling at the moment."[2]

Or consider the Federal Trade Commission report that concluded movie studios systematically target teens under 17 when marketing R-rated movies: "Internal studio documents show that MGM/UA marketers went to great lengths to orchestrate a word-of-mouth campaign to make sure underage teens were aware of their movie (the R-rated *Disturbing Behavior*)."[3] A *Los Angeles Times* expose of Hollywood's obsession with marketing to teens describes how teens were organized into teams and paid to hand-out bumper stickers, posters, and bracelets promoting the movie. Teen teams from New York, Philadelphia, and Atlanta targeted popular roller-blade spots, summer sports, cheerleading, band, and drill team camps, and all-age nightclubs that attract huge teen crowds.

The *Los Angeles Times* article also revealed that Disney's Miramax studio planned to distribute fliers and posters of a 1997 R-rated movie to dozens of youth organizations, including the Girl and Boy Scouts, and a Paramount Pictures memo outlined plans for buying television and radio ads targeted at the 12- to 24-year-old audience to promote their R-rated film, *The General's Daughter*.[4]

Media Content

The American Medical Association reports that, in one year, the average child spends about 1,500 hours in front of the television compared to 900 hours in school. Teens are exposed to an estimated 3,000 ads a day.[5] And 65 per cent of U.S. teens have a television in their bedroom.[6]

What are children watching in those 1,500, mostly unsupervised, hours?

■ TV's early evening "Family Hour" contains more than eight sexual incidents per hour, four times more than in 1976.[7]

◄ Each year, teens view nearly 15,000 sexual references, innuendoes, and jokes. Only 170 of these will deal with abstinence, birth control, STDs, or pregnancy.[8]

◄ References to gay sex rose 2,650 per cent.[9]

They've viewed a lot of sexual content. What are they learning?

According to a recent article in the *Journal of Adolescent Health*, many teens are learning that the pursuit of sex is relentless and exploitative. Sex is often portrayed as nothing more than a sporting event that amounts only to innocent fun with no real emotional or physical consequences.[10]

The article goes on to describe the harmful effects of prolonged exposure to such "erotic" media. Teens can:

■ Accept the perception that "everybody's doing it."

■ Lose hope for sexual exclusivity.

■ View promiscuity as the "natural state."

■ View sexual inactivity as a health risk.

■ Become cynical about love.

■ Believe that one can achieve superior sexual pleasure without affection toward your partner.

■ View marriage as confining.

■ View having and raising a family as unattractive.

Sexual *inactivity* is a health risk? Promiscuity is the natural state? These are pretty blatant "cons." Such misinformation confuses and misleads teens. Just like the sexual con artist who carefully grooms his target with language cons (lines), bribes, or flattery, many media conglomerates are carefully "grooming" their target audience – youth – with attractive but misleading information about sex, dating, and relationships. Misinformation and lies like these lead some teens down a dangerous path of unhealthy and harmful relationships and experiences.

Why do media and advertisers target teens? Consider these numbers:

■ According to the 2000 U.S. Census, there are 31.6 million 12- to 19-year-olds in the U. S., the largest generation ever.

■ According to Teen Research Unlimited, in 2000, U.S. teens spent an estimated $105 billion and influenced their parents to spend another $48 billion.

■ 34 per cent of teen purchases are clothing, and another 22 per cent – approximately $30 billion – is spent on entertainment (CDs, movie tickets, video games, etc.).

Today's teen population has a large amount of disposable income. Media conglomerates know this and purposefully target this money. Their goal is to capture the attention of youth long enough to promote and sell their products. One of the most effective ways to capture teens' attention amid the "clutter and noise" of other advertisements and programming is to use provocative sexual imagery.[11] Often the sexual imagery and stories in the media are,

at the least, one-dimensional and, at the worst, dangerous exaggerations or lies. Many teens are literally "buying" these lies.

Counteracting Media Messages

So what can we do to counteract the media's influence on teens' attitudes toward sexual behavior? How can we protect and reclaim the moral goodness and happiness of youth? Here are some suggestions:

■ Take every opportunity to tell youth and model for them, your values and beliefs regarding the purpose of friendship, dating, marriage, and sex.

■ Teach youth that the best preparation for marriage and family is learning friendship skills. Teach youth how to be a good friend and how to have healthy boundaries with friends.

■ Find out what kinds of media your youth are consuming and do your homework – listen to their music, look up song lyrics on the web, watch their TV shows, preview videos. Check out some of the websites listed in this chapter.

■ Say "no" to inappropriate media. Tell youth why it's wrong or harmful!

■ Teach youth critical thinking skills that enable them to evaluate media and compare media messages about sex, dating, and relationships to your family values.

■ Create opportunities to practice critical thinking. For example, watch a TV show, music video, or movie together.

Have teens look for and name any of the nine grooming tactics seen in this show or movie. Discuss how relationships in real life would be damaged by these sexual con games.

We can help our youth learn the skills they need – skills that will enable them to think critically, reflect, and reject lies about sex. These skills will enable them to create and maintain healthy friendships and good relationships – the kinds of relationships that respect and protect innocence and purity – the kinds of relationships that will enable our children to treat each other with respect and dignity!

Some helpful web sites are:

- Movie reviews for parents – www.screenit.com

- Focus on the Family: Plugged-In Magazine – www.family.org/pplace/pi/

- National Abstinence Clearinghouse – www.abstinence.com

- Song lyrics – www.lyrics.com

- Get Net Wise – www.getnetwise.org

- Girls and Boys Town resources – www.girlsandboystown.org

1 *Plugged In* magazine, December, 2001.

2 Ibid.

3 "Hollywood Took Aim at Teens by Using Freebies, Fliers Ads," *The Los Angeles Times,* Sept, 2000.

4 Ibid.

5 From PBS documentary, *The Merchants of Cool,* 2000.

6 Kaiser Family Foundation.

7 Strasburger and Donnerstein, *Children, Adolescents and the Media: Issues and Solutions,* Pediatrics Journal, 1999.

8 Ibid.

9 Parents Television Council.

10 D. Zillman, *Influences of Unrestrained Access to Erotica on Adolescents and Young Adults' Dispositions Towards Sexuality,* Journal of Adolescent Health, August, 2000.

11 Sut Jhally, in the video *Dreamworlds II,* 1995, Media Education Foundation.

Emotional Grooming
and Sexual Harassment

Grooming tactics can often be forms of sexual harassment. When teaching teens how to recognize and avoid emotional grooming, it is also important to help teens understand what sexual harassment is – how to recognize it and how to report it. Protecting students from sexual harassment in schools is the law.

Two Types of Harassment

According to the Department of Education Office for Civil Rights there are two types of sexual harassment that can occur in a school setting: quid pro quo and hostile environment.

Quid pro quo harassment – This is harassment of a student by a school employee. In this case, a school employee "...causes a student to believe that he or she must submit to unwelcome sexual conduct in order to participate in a school program or activity" and/or leads a student to believe that an educational decision will be "...based on whether or not the student submits to unwelcome sexual conduct." For example, a teacher threatens to fail a student if she reports the teacher's unwelcome sexual advances.

Hostile environment harassment – This is defined as severe, persistent, or pervasive unwelcome sexual conduct by a school employee, another student, or even someone visiting the school that creates a threatening, abusive, or intimidating environment. This type of harassment can be so upsetting that it negatively affects student(s)' "ability to participate in or benefit from an education program or activity." For example, a female student daily sends sexual notes or pictures, makes unwelcome sexual comments, and grabs at a male student in biology class. The target skips class to avoid the harassment but his grades begin to drop.

Author and researcher on this subject, Dr. Nan Stein, describes sexual harassment as "unwanted or unwelcome sexual behavior which interferes with your right to get an education or to participate in school activities. In school, sexual harassment may result from words or conduct of a sexual nature that offend, stigmatize, demean, frighten or threaten you because of your sex."

Research compiled by Dr. Stein found the following examples of sexual harassment in school settings:

- Touching, pinching, or grabbing body parts

- Being cornered or leaned over

- Sending sexual notes or pictures

- Writing sexual graffiti

- Making suggestive or sexual gestures, looks, comments, jokes, or noises

- Spreading sexual rumors or making sexual propositions

- Pulling off your own or someone else's clothes

- Being forced to kiss someone or do something sexual

- Attempted rape and rape

Dr. Stein also makes it clear that the target(s) and the perpetrator(s) do not need to agree that sexual harassment is occurring. The target, or others observing or feeling the effects of a hostile environment define sexual harassment, not the harasser. For example, every morning before school, Sam and Carla make out in the hallway. Other students and teachers are uncomfortable and offended by this public display of affection. Sam and Carla may not realize it, but their behavior is creating a hostile environment.

Is It Harassment?

Are sexual con games the same thing as sexual harassment? In many cases, emotional grooming and sexual con games are sexual harassment. Remember, sexual con games are the means by which an emotional groomer attempts to seduce, coerce or "con" another into sexual activity. The groomer could be an adult, as in quid pro quo sexual harassment, or another youth as in hostile environment harassment. Each of the nine grooming tactics and language cons is exactly what Dr. Stein describes as harassment – an action intended to "offend, stigmatize, demean, frighten or threaten" someone into some sort of sexual behavior.

What is the difference between sexual harassment and bullying? There are two kinds of harassment – sexual and nonsexual. Bullying is generally nonsexual harassment. It can be just as hurtful and creates just as hostile and dangerous an environment as sexual harassment. Both kinds of harassment are wrong. Both create big problems for youth in school. No harassment of any kind should be allowed in school. For more on how to remedy this problem, check out *Protecting Students from Harassment and Hate Crimes: A Guide for Schools* (1999) U.S. Department of Education Office for Civil Rights, or download it for free at www.ed.gov/pubs/Harassment.

What does the law require? According to Dr. Stein, "School district officials are legally responsible to guarantee an education for all students in a safe environment which is free from sexual harassment." Title IX, enforced by the Office for Civil Rights, mandates that when school officials become aware of any form of sexual harassment they are, by law, required to take immediate steps to stop the harassment and to prevent it from happening again. School districts and individual schools should have written policies and set procedures regarding sexual harassment. Title IX requires that each school district appoint a coordinator to oversee the district's compliance with this federal regulation. When it comes to sexual harassment, school officials have legal responsibilities and students have rights. For more information, go to the Office for Civil Rights web page, www.ed.gov/offices/OCR.

Prevention Strategies

How do you prevent sexual harassment? Some good prevention strategies include:

Develop a "zero tolerance" policy on sexual harassment. The policy needs to specifically name the behaviors that will not be tolerated (see list on previous page) and the consequences for engaging in sexual harassment. All students, teachers, staff, and parents need to be informed of the policy and how it will be enforced.

Provide training for teachers, school staff, and even adult volunteers. The training should include a clear and concise definition of sexual harassment, the school's legal responsibilities and students' rights, what sexual harassment in schools looks like and sounds like, how to teach to sexual harassment when it happens, and what the appropriate response and consequence should be. If every adult in the school is "on the same page" when it comes to teaching to this behavior, youth will get a clear and consistent message that sexual harassment will not be tolerated and that you intend to provide a safe learning environment. A sample outline of such a workshop for teachers and administrators closes this chapter.

Teach students how to identify and report sexual harassment. Let students know the specific inappropriate sexual behaviors that will not be tolerated and what the consequences will be for anyone who chooses to engage in such behaviors.

Sample Sexual Harassment Workshop
for Teachers and Administrators

Pre-Workshop Preparation

If time permits, about two weeks before your scheduled workshop send participants a Pre-Workshop Survey and a cover letter explaining the survey, which should address such issues as school climate and knowledge of school policy on harassment. The U.S. Department of Education Office for Civil Rights offers such a survey on its web site, www.ed.gov/pubs/Harassment. Click on Appendix B: Protocols and Checklists.

Request that participants complete the survey and return it to you before the workshop. You can use the information gathered from these surveys to make yourself familiar with the particular areas of concern participants are facing. The information can also help you tailor the workshop to fit their needs.

Workshop Outline

1. Present or make reference to information gathered from the pre-workshop survey.

2. Define relevant terms and topics.

    a. Sexual harassment

    b. Quid pro quo harassment

    c. Hostile environment harassment

    d. Title IX – specifically what the law requires of schools

3. Discuss what is happening in schools.

    a. Demonstrate the kinds of inappropriate sexual behavior and sexual harassment occurring in schools across the country by presenting information from current research and surveys.

        Hostile Hallways: The AAUW Survey on Sexual Harassment in America's Schools (1993), (800)225-9998, ext. 246.

        Secrets in Public: Sexual Harassment in Our Schools (1993) Stein, Marshall, and Tropp, (781) 283-2510.

    b. If available, show video, *Flirting or Hurting? Sexual Harassment in Schools* (1996), 57 minutes, (800) 228-4630.

4. Discuss how and why we should respond, teach to, and prevent these inappropriate behaviors.

   a. Ask participants to review and discuss the school's current sexual harassment policy and implementation. Have copies of the sexual harassment policy available for reference. Allow time for participants to name any problems with current policy or implementation.

   b. Define "skills." Describe how teaching students skills can help youth treat others with respect. Show specific skills that can be taught to enable youth to handle sexual harassment, such as How to Identify and Report Sexual Harassment, How to Ask for Help, How to Recognize/Avoid a Groomer, How to Have Good Peer Relations, How to Set and Maintain Good Boundaries, etc. (For skills, see pages 73-75.)

   c. Present Effective Praise and Proactive Teaching as methods for preventing sexual harassment. Present Corrective Teaching as a method for immediately responding and teaching to inappropriate behaviors. (See Chapter 9 for descriptions of these teaching techniques.)

   d. Have the group discuss and list appropriate consequences for various inappropriate behaviors. Break into groups to name and discuss what would work in their setting.

   e. Discuss how to educate and involve parents and how parents and teachers can cooperate, share information, and work to prevent inappropriate or harmful behaviors.

   f. Allow time for participants to create and act out a role-play that demonstrates a problem behavior observed in their school and how to use Corrective or Proactive Teaching to address it.

5

Emotional Grooming and Dating Violence

One dangerous potential and prevalent result of emotional grooming is violence in relationships. Some groomers learn how to manipulate others by watching violent and abusive relationships

in their own families. Such groomers are likely to re-enact what they've seen in their families in their own dating relationships. Other groomers get the message that force or violence in dating relationships is okay from the media they consume. Sexualized violence is becoming more commonplace in teen movies and music. Wherever the messages are coming from, many teens are taking them in, and using violence as a way to get what they want in dating relationships.

Dating violence is exactly what it sounds like – physical, sexual, verbal, or emotional abuse or violence that occurs between dating partners. Unfortunately, dating violence is on the rise, especially among teens.

The August, 2001, issue of the *Journal of the American Medical Association* reported that, according to surveys conducted with over 4,000 public schools students, one in every

five high school girls had been physically or sexually abused by a dating partner. Jay G. Silverman, of Harvard University's School of Public Health and lead author of this study, reported, "A disturbing number of adolescent boys have adopted attitudes that men are entitled to control their girlfriends through violence."[1]

Scope of the Problem

Consider these statistics:

- The U.S. Department of Justice reports that young women, ages 16-24, experience the highest rates of violence by current or former intimate partners.[2]

- 40 per cent of girls 14-17 report knowing someone who has been hit or beaten by her boyfriend.[3]

- One-third of high school and college students experience violence in an intimate relationship during their dating years.[4]

- According to community-based surveys, more than half of adolescent girls who reported being sexually assaulted were assaulted while on dates.[5]

However, it is not only young men who are using violence in dating relationships. Growing numbers of young women are also using violence to control their dating partners. According to recent estimates by the U.S. Centers for Disease Control and Prevention, 22 per cent of high school students are victims of nonsexual dating violence, **with girls only slightly more likely to be victims.** Other research conducted by the Massachusetts Department of Education in 1999 found that:

- 18 per cent of all girls and 7 per cent of all boys had been physically or sexually hurt by a date.

- 16 per cent of all girls and 6 per cent of all boys have had sexual contact against their will.

Is It Grooming?

Using violence to control, manipulate, threaten, or coerce someone is always wrong and always harmful. And it is also a grooming tactic. Remember, emotional grooming is a process that is used to coerce, manipulate or control someone else. Dating violence is controlling, manipulative, threatening, and coercive. Dating violence and abuse are forms of emotional grooming.

Dating violence and abuse have obvious physical dangers – bumps and bruises, black eyes, broken limbs. But they can also present some other very real and serious psychological and social repercussions for teens. Girls who were victims of dating violence and abuse were:

- About 8-9 times more likely to have attempted suicide in the previous year.

- 4-6 times more likely to have ever been pregnant.

- 3-5 times more likely to have used cocaine.

- 3-4 times more likely to have used unhealthy dieting methods such as laxatives or vomiting.[6]

In some ways teens may be more susceptible to becoming victims of dating violence than adults. Many teens lack the social skills and life experience that would help them recognize grooming behaviors as abusive. Some young people may mistake jealousy, possessiveness, and controlling behaviors as true love and concern. And sometimes, teens are just reluctant to ask for help. Unsure of whom to go to, fearing judgment, condemnation, or loss of a relationship, they remain silent.

How to Help

There are four important things adults can do to help teens avoid any kind of sexual con game, whether it be emotional grooming, dating violence, sexual abuse, or sexual harassment. We can:

- Educate teens on each of these issues.

- Teach teens skills.

- Teach teens boundaries.

- Create safe environments for teens.

Providing good information on these topics can help teens gain a clear understanding of not only what is dangerous and unhealthy in dating and other relationships, but also what is healthy and appropriate. Such information can help them learn how to recognize and avoid unhealthy and dangerous situations and people, as well as help them make better decisions about relationships in general.

But information alone is not enough. We must also provide teens with the practical, "how- to's" of relationships. Teens need all kinds of relationship skills. Communication skills, refusal skills, critical thinking skills, problem solving skills – these skills and more can help teens practice avoiding what is unhealthy while learning how to create and maintain healthy and positive relationships. Skills provide teens with the practical behaviors that can help them interact in positive and healthy ways with peers and adults alike.

One very important set of skills teens must learn if they want healthy friendships and relationships are boundary-setting skills. Good and appropriate boundaries are essential for any healthy relationship. Teaching teens how to create and maintain healthy boundaries will provide them with tools that can help them have happier, healthier, and safer relationships throughout their lives. See Chapters 8 and 9 and the lesson plans in Chapter 10 for more on how to teach social skills and boundaries to teens.

And finally, if we want to help teens avoid harmful relationships and achieve healthy relationships, we must "raise the bar." We must establish firm and clear guidelines for acceptable and unacceptable behavior. We must never tolerate, ignore or engage in any sort of grooming, sexual abuse, sexual harassment, or dating violence. We must be clear regarding the specific expectations they will be held to, and then we must hold them to it. For more information on what those behavioral expectations should be and how to teach them to teens, see Chapter 8.

It is important to note that although abuse most often occurs in a home, the location where physical abuse is most often reported is in the schools. Of teen dating violence that occurs at school, 84 per cent involves some sort of physical violence.[7] Since teens spend most of their day at school, it is essential for school personnel to examine how to address this growing problem.

The Massachusetts Department of Education has been a frontrunner in studying and addressing how to respond to teen dating violence. Following, you'll find its sample written policy for addressing teen dating violence in school.

1 Journal of American Medical Association, August, 2001.

2 U.S. Dept. of Justice. Violence by Intimates, NCJ-167237, March, 1998. Washington D.C.: Bureau of Justice Statistics.

3 Children Now/Kaiser Permanente Poll, December, 1995.

4 Wolfe, L. R., "Girl stabs boy at school": Girls and the Cycle of Violence. Women's Health Issues, 4 (2) p. 111, 1994.

5 Ibid.

6 Journal of American Medical Association, August, 2001.

7 Updated Guidelines for Schools on Addressing Teen Dating Violence, article, www.doe.mass.edu.

Addressing Teen Dating Violence

Updated Guidelines for Schools – Massachusetts Department of Education
Sample Written Policy Chart

Behaviors That Are Not Allowed	Consequence
Verbal, Nonverbal or Written • Use of putdowns, insults, name calling, swearing, or offensive language • Screaming or yelling at another • Making threats, being intimidating or getting friends to threaten or scare another	**First Offense** Verbal warning/ Education **Repeat Offense** Teacher student conference Send to office/detention
Physical • Hitting, punching, pinching, pushing, shoving, grabbing, slapping, kicking, choking, pulling hair, biting, throwing things, arm twisting • Intimidation, blocking exits, punching walls, knocking things around • Damaging or destroying another's property • Restraining, pinning someone to the wall, blocking their movements	**First Offense** Detention/Education/ Suspension **Repeat Offense** Detention plus Diversion program/ Suspension/ Dangerousness assessment
Using Weapons	Suspension/Expulsion
Stalking	Suspension/Expulsion
Sexual • Name calling, such as slut, bitch, fag • Cat calls or other offensive noises or whistling • Spreading sexual gossip or graffiti • Comments about a person's body or unwanted verbal or written sexual comments • Staring or leering with sexual overtones, sexual gestures	**First Offense** Detention/Education/ Suspension **Repeat Offense** Suspension/Psychological assessment
Forcing obscene materials on others	Suspension/Expulsion
Pulling off or lifting clothes to expose private parts	Suspension/Expulsion
Rape or attempted rape	Suspension/Expulsion

Administrator	Parents/ Caretaker	Referral	Document
Yes, if appropriate	Yes, if appropriate	Yes, if appropriate	Yes
Inform	Inform	Dating or Other Violence Prevention Counselor	Yes
Must inform	Parent conference	Dating or Other Violence Prevention Counselor	Yes
Repeat Offense Must inform	**Repeat Offense** Parent conference	School Security Police	
Must inform	Must inform	Police	Yes
Must inform	Must inform	Police	Yes
Must inform	Parent conference	Sexual Harassment Counselor	Yes
Must inform	Parent conference before admittance	Dating Violence or Rape Counselor School Security	Yes
Must inform	Must inform	Police	Yes
Must inform	Must inform	Police	Yes
Must inform	Must inform	Police	Yes

Emotional Grooming and Sexual Abuse

6

Sexual abuse is an extremely complicated problem. It is possible that you may be the first adult to discover that one of the youth you work with has been sexually abused. It also is possible that

this youth will trust you enough to disclose what happened. It is more likely, however, that after years of emotional grooming where the youth has been successfully conned into sexual activity, he or she will hold fast to the "secret." The sexual abuse may come to light only because of the keen eyes and ears of the adults who deal with youth on a frequent basis.

Many studies indicate that a lack of adequate knowledge and appropriate sexual information, on the part of both youth and adults, compounds the problem of sexual abuse. All youth need information and education about values, and a positive attitude that allows them to identify and avoid sexual abuse.

People who work with youth should be aware of the signs of sexual abuse and have an understanding of its impact. For those

youth who already have been abused, healing is possible only with the help of educated, concerned, and caring adults. That's why the following information is included.

The Emotional Grooming Process

Some youth, especially those who have been sexually abused, seem to be consciously willing to engage in promiscuous sexual activity. It may not be their fault; it may be the way they have learned to relate to others. Many of these youth have been victims of years of emotional grooming. That is, they have been seduced or "conned" into participating. (Although emotional grooming in this context applies to sexually abused youth, the same tactics are used by sexual con artists in a much shorter, and often more intense, time frame.)

In sexually abusive situations, the process of emotional grooming can begin at any age, but usually starts when the child is not yet able to fully understand the impact of sexual behavior or not yet capable of giving informed consent. The abuser could be a person who is the same age as the child, an older adolescent, or in many cases, an adult. The child may experience pleasurable sexual sensations while the abuse is taking place, but he or she is incapable of understanding sexual feelings or sexual behavior in the same way adults do. Children cannot understand the full psychological and social impact of the sexual behavior in which they are engaging. And, most commonly, a child is not developmentally mature enough to resist the inappropriate sexual advances of an abuser.

Many abusers rely on the advantage of being older and stronger than their targets to seduce, lure, or threaten them into engaging in sexual behavior. The authority and power of the abuser, along with the child's lack of maturity and subordinate position, allow the abuser to coerce the child into sexual compliance. Basically, sex is being forced on a child who lacks emotional, physical, and cognitive development.

Emotional grooming of sexually abused youth usually falls into two categories: reward behaviors and punishing behaviors.

Rewards may include:

■ Gifts

■ Emotional nurturance and closeness from another person

■ Special privileges or getting out of something that other youth have to do

■ Overt bribery – *"Let me touch your breasts, and I'll buy you a new outfit."*

Punishing behaviors may include:

■ Psychological intimidation – *"If you don't have sex with me, I'll sneak into your room at night and rape you."*

■ Hitting, slapping, pulling hair, teasing

■ Direct physical force

Possible Indicators of Sexual Abuse

Knowing the behavioral characteristics of sexually abused youth may help you identify a victim. Remember, most victims, especially male victims, will not readily disclose their abuse. Many victims are fearful of telling because of threatened retribution from the abuser. Be sensitive and cautious when attempting to help a victim reveal suspected abuse. Keep in mind that it may take some time for the "whole story" to be revealed.

The following behaviors may suggest that sexual abuse has occurred:

Wrestling and tickling – These can be considered normal childhood behaviors, but they also can take on sexual overtones. Wrestling and tickling can be painful or humiliating, or cause discomfort to the weaker person who is on the receiving end. Wrestling, tickling, or roughhousing can be sexually stimulating and can lead to more explicit sexual activities.

Obscene language – Youth, especially young children, imitate what they see and hear. A child who uses obscene or sexually explicit language may be repeating words and phrases used during their grooming and sexual abuse.

Frequent touching – Although some touching is healthy, a sexually abused child will touch adults or other youth more frequently, and often in inappropriate ways. A sexually abused child may attempt to touch others' genitalia or touch in a way that usually leads to more sexually intimate behavior. Touching can be a subtle form of foreplay. A youth who frequently touches adults or children may have learned this behavior from an abuser.

Wearing sexually suggestive clothing – Extremely tight or revealing clothing can be interpreted as a "come-on" to the opposite sex. This kind of dress may have been expected or even controlled by the abuser. The sexually abused child may or may not realize that wearing suggestive clothing often draws negative or sexual attention.

Self-mutilation – tattoos, cigarette burns, hickeys, cuts on the arms. This is a sign of a loss of self-respect and the powerlessness youth feel regarding what happens to them.

Combination of violence and sexuality in artwork or schoolwork – Youth express themselves in words, art, and play. Pay attention to subtle signs.

Overt sexual acting out toward adults – Be cautious with a youth who appears "too friendly." Many sexually abused youth will associate sexual behavior with adult acceptance and caring. You have to explain and maintain your boundaries, too.

Extreme fear or revulsion when touched by an adult of either sex – Youth who have been sexually abused may not associate a nurturing touch with pleasure or safety. Touching often has been foreplay for them or has eventually led to a sexually abusive situation. Being touched affectionately by an adult may not be viewed as pleasurable by the youth; it may be viewed as threatening or even terrifying.

Running away – Youth either run away from something or to something. They may be running away from a sexually abusive environment or to a place they think is safe. Many times, running away will result in sexual or drug-oriented behavior.

Treatment

There are specific therapeutic strategies that adults can utilize in treating youth who have been sexually abused. The most important techniques are consistent teaching, counseling, and genuine support. Some youth, however, may need additional help such as that provided by specially trained therapists.

Therapy provides youth with opportunities to express and clarify thoughts and to work through painful feelings. The following types of treatment are available to targets of sexual abuse and their families: individual therapy, group therapy, and inpatient treatment.

Individual therapy usually occurs on an outpatient basis with a clinical social worker, clinical psychologist, or psychiatrist. Group therapy is especially helpful with teenage targets. Treatment gives them a chance to overcome some of their feelings of isolation (*"No one has ever experienced anything as bad as I have."*) and to eliminate the secrecy associated with sexual abuse. In a group, they have the chance to receive support for their feelings and rights, and see that others have learned to act upon these feelings in a positive way. Youth also learn interpersonal skills that help make them less vulnerable to being victimized again.

Inpatient treatment is sometimes required for youth who are at great risk for self-destructive behavior. Hospitalization can provide the safety and medical supervision required for youth who are temporarily overwhelmed by feelings associated with their abuse and possible severe mental illness. The desired outcome of inpatient treatment is the return of the youth to an environment that is free of abuse.

Most sexually abused youth need a chance to resolve many complex issues that are associated with their victimization. Among the more common issues are:

Believability – The youth who attempted to disclose the abuse and wasn't believed may need repeated assurance that he or she will be believed now. The youth also needs to know that disclosing the abuse was the right thing to do.

Guilt and responsibility – Frequently, the abuser will blame the youth for the abuse, saying the youth was seductive and "asked for it." If the abuser was a member of the family, the youth also may be blamed by other family members for breaking up or bringing shame upon the family. The youth needs to be reassured regularly that he or she is not responsible for the abuse. The target must know that all aspects of the abuse were the abuser's fault.

Body image and physical safety – Sexually abused youth need to discuss how they feel about their bodies. Many think that their bodies caused the abuse and punish themselves accordingly. They also may need to realize that as a consequence of their abuse, they use their bodies to gain inappropriate attention and rewards. They need to be taught how to respect and care for their bodies. Such supportive learning helps combat the "damaged goods" feeling of being a sexual abuse target.

Secrecy and sharing – By discussing what behaviors and thoughts can be shared or be kept private, the youth learns that relationships can be chosen, instead of forced upon her or him.

Anger – The youth needs to honestly explore her or his angry feelings about the abuser. During this process of exploration, youth can learn new and appropriate skills to recognize and express anger.

Powerlessness – The youth needs to learn how to regain a sense of control of her or his own life, rather than being controlled by abusers and others. On the other hand, the youth needs to learn appropriate limits, so as to not overdo it and try to control everything.

Shame – Sexually abused youth often are left feeling contaminated, as if there is something fundamentally and essentially wrong with them. The worst thing that can happen to them, therefore, is for someone else to see or know their basic flaw. Sexually abused youth must own and work through such feelings of shame. This is possible with your understanding and care.

Your Attitude and Behavior

Many adults find it difficult to talk openly with students about sex. When the subject involves sexual abuse, adults find it an even more formidable task. Many adults choose to avoid the issue altogether, apparently hoping that someone else, someone more qualified or comfortable with the subject, will tackle it. When a person charged with helping children takes this approach, the youth will not learn the proper lessons about sexuality.

Sexual abuse is abhorrent. There's no question about that. It violates a child emotionally, morally, and physically. We adults may feel disgust and rage toward abusers and sympathy for targets. But no matter what we feel, we cannot lose sight of the task that confronts us. It is crucial that we, as caregivers, learn how to set our emotions aside so that we can begin teaching our youth.

The first place to begin is to learn to treat sexuality and relationship education as a necessary part of our students' overall education. Of course, any discussion of sex, especially the issue of sexual abuse, should be serious and sensitive. But it need not be frightening, condemning, or condescending. A discussion about sex is neither a lecture on morals nor a forum for slang and innuendoes. Sex education gives our children valuable knowledge that will help them learn how to make healthy decisions regarding future sexual behavior and prevent them from making drastic mistakes. The essence of your teaching is that sex is a natural topic for discussion and should be discussed before youth find out about it through their own sexual experimentation. Ironically, many sexually abused youth say they had never been told what sexual abuse was, let alone that it could ever happen to them. Therefore, education is a key to having youth learn what is and is not sexually appropriate.

Be honest and share information. Unfortunately, some adults think that they will unduly upset students by allowing them to know that terrible things such as sexual abuse occur. They think that it would be much better to shelter youth from this reality. Similarly, youth may not want to disclose information regarding abuse because they think the adults will reject their reports as foolish. As youth see adults avoid the topic, they too learn to hide or avoid talking about it. A cycle of avoidance is developed and the secret of sexual abuse continues. It is healthier to give youth as much information as you can about the tragedies of sexual abuse.

Be open about discussions of both sexual abuse and positive relationships. Negative descriptions of people or relationships need to be balanced with positive descriptions. In other words, youth need not be fearful that everyone is an abuser; they need to know that there also are many caring people with whom they can build healthy relationships. If youth learn both the "good" and "bad," they form a much better perspective on sexuality and will be less likely to be alarmed by any discussion of sexual abuse.

Teach your students the difference between "good" secrets and "bad" secrets. This may take a great deal of time because it involves teaching students how to identify emotions and feelings. In other words, teach about the emotional burden that comes with a bad secret and the good feeling that goes with knowing a good secret that later will be shared with others. For example, a "bad" secret is when a student is frightened or conned into never telling anyone that Daddy and she have a "special" sexual relationship. A "good" secret is when a student knows there is a surprise birthday party planned for one of her friends. There is an enormous difference in the impact these two secrets have on a child's life, yet the child may not be able to distinguish between them. When a youth starts displaying behaviors that signal withdrawal into secret relationships, it may indicate some type of abusive relationship.

Speak in even, matter-of-fact voice tones. When an adult is dealing with a child who has been sexually abused, the child may pick up verbal cues that remind him or her of the abuser's behaviors. Overly emotional, intense behavior may trigger the same type of behavior in a sexually abused child. One of the primary skills you should develop is the ability to handle sexual discussions in a way that promotes openness and seriousness, but does not intimate either sexual promiscuity or strong aversions to the discussions. This also means that you should not talk to students on "their level." Using anatomically correct language provides children with proper sexual terms. This will require a great deal of teaching on your part because much, or all, of the child's sexual knowledge will have come either from a parent – possibly an abusive one – or from a peer group. This also means that youth will "slip up" occasionally. It is best to gently correct them and let them continue. Any strong reaction of disapproval or disgust at their terminology may work against you; the child may use slang terms purposely to avoid the truth or to change the subject. This is not to say that you should continually tolerate slang, cussing, or any other inappropriate verbal statements; you should constantly teach appropriate language. Any shock value in your response may give the child a recourse to use against you in the future. It is important to use correct language consis-

tently; therefore, it is wise to practice what you're going to say.

Believe what your students tell you. Tell them you are going to trust them. Many times before, people may have told a youth they would believe what he or she said, and then didn't. The youth may have felt betrayed or rejected instead – especially if he or she told someone about being sexually abused.

The way you respond can be an appropriate model for your students. It can help youth who have been sexually abused learn to go beyond their abuse and start to live healthful, constructive lives. It won't be easy. There are numerous problems to face along the way. You may become depressed or angry at times. Sometimes, you may not know what to do next. You may feel enmeshed in the student's problems. Share your feelings with your co-workers. It is likely they will have similar feelings and emotions. Talk with specialists in the field of sexual abuse. They may give you some insight and suggestions that will help you out. Above all else, believe that the service you are providing to sexually abused youth is bringing some hope back into their lives.

The Many Masks of the Emotional Groomer

Sexual con artists wear "masks" to hide their true intentions. These masks can't be seen like real masks can. They are invisible disguises meant to keep a con artist's games from being known or discovered. These masks come in the form of words, behaviors, or mind games, like making a target feel afraid or guilty. But if youth learn to look closely, they will see that behind each sexual con artist's mask is someone who wants to use and manipulate them. Targets also wear masks to cover up the shame, fear, or humiliation they feel.

Teenagers who participated in the Unmasking Sexual Con Games curriculum wrote the following passages. The masks and the excerpts you will see in this chapter were created by them as part of a classroom project to illustrate how they felt about being involved in a sexual con game. The students made the masks out of papier-mâché or plaster, and painted them to reflect certain feelings and emotions. They then wrote about what the masks meant. This classroom activity is described as an optional session in Chapter 10.

The following stories are real. Some youth were targets; some were sexual con artists; some were both. Listen carefully to what they have to say. Listen to the pain they have caused in others or have felt themselves.

What Girls Said

My mask is a groomer who has blue hair – a cold-hearted, red face – angry of being caught, smug look – knowing that he got what he wanted. My mask would say, "Hey baby, would you like to jump in bed with me?" Two hours later: "Ha, ha, I got my way!"

My mask represents a groomer showing his many colors: overpowering, slyness, evilness.

My mask would say, "I'm a great guy. All the girls like me. You'd be missing out if you're not with me." My mask hides the darkness in his life and having low self-esteem and being paranoid about others finding out about him.

My mask symbolizes no feelings. The pain and the hurt is shown by the black on the inside. And now I don't feel anything anymore because I've been hurt so much that the black pain is coming through on the outside.

My mask is a guy who says, "I have been keeping my eyes on you. I knew when I first saw you that you were the one for me." Groomers are the persons who do not use their own personalities but they use masks to be someone else.

My mask symbolizes the darkness and hurt feelings that a target goes through when she is taken advantage of. If it could talk, it would scream "No!" so that the violator will know that no game is going to be played with me. My mask also hides the fear that I will be used again. Hiding the hurt I feel from being used the first time. And the shame, not knowing if it was my fault.

My mask is all black and the face is red. This symbolizes someone in such pain and being so hurt that the pain took over. My mask would say all the feelings that it had inside. It would let others know that this is not the way you should feel. You shouldn't let people to get you into these situations. Look what it has done. It is hiding the truth about a lot of things. There is a lost person that wants to fight back.

My mask would say, "I thought he loved me." He made me experience feelings, but he wasn't feeling the same. My mask is hiding the true person she really is, her shame. The eyes are closed because she doesn't want people to see the window to her soul.

My mask is a mold of myself. The color represents how my life has been divided into worlds. The red shows the pain and the black shows the loneliness and the white shows the acceptance. The teardrops represent how hurt I've been in both areas. My mask hides the pain, hurt, and fright from the world. The uncertain child that could never grow up and be herself.

My mask is a symbol of violation, the dark represents a deep dark heart. I do not like it when I am violated; it makes me feel like a helpless child with nowhere to turn. My mask would say, "Help, get away, I'm telling." It would say that in a voice that has a crying scream. My mask is hiding me; it's a face someone put on me that has dirty feelings and behind it is a person who wants to love. But it is hard to love anyone anymore and to even get close to anyone!

My mask is split into different colors. The colors are symbols of all the different things that I felt when being violated. The thick black lines that separate colors mean that the feelings are so separate that they stand alone and are very strong. The black eyes stand for blindness and confusion, the disability to see exactly what is being thrown at the target and to see what this will lead to. The mouth is in the position to kiss, which shows the feeling of needing to be cared for. You'll sacrifice your feelings and self-worth. The eyebrows slanting mean that this target knows something is wrong. My mask hides confusion, hurt confidence, trapped feelings, indecision.

My mask has bright colors to show how targets may present themselves on the outside. There are dark tears coming from this person's eyes. Their eyes are black – they can't see a way out. Many colors around the face, trying to get out, distorted nose, distorted picture.

What Guys Said

These masks I wear are just cover-ups for what I really feel. It gets me what I want. I build false relationships. I lie. I lose trust in myself and I can never trust others. I just want things my way and to have no one know how much I hurt inside.

You hurt emotionally and physically. You wear your mask so much you don't know who you really are anymore. You don't know how to get better. And no one wants to be your friend.

I hurt myself by getting deeper into the grooming stuff. It is so hard to get out. It just causes you to have grief and can get you locked up if you get caught. You hurt others by using these tactics on them, taking their feelings and respect away. I wish I had never started saying and doing all those things but now I'm trapped and I have a reputation.

The mask I wore said, "Hey baby, I think you look real good. Maybe me and you could get to know each other a little better. Huh, say how 'bout you give me your number and I can give you a call later." These are all the lines I use.

My mask tried to intimidate the girl to go out or do something with me. I would put on the pressure. If I didn't get what I wanted, I'd get very angry. Even though I would hurt people, I knew anger would work and I could get what I want.

My mask had anger and status. My mask tried hard to get what it wanted. If it did not, it got very mad. My mask didn't like it when he used his best bait and you still got away.

First, I would use flattery. Then I would use status. And if that didn't work, I would use insecurity. "What's up marvelous? I'm GQ. Yeah you might have seen me playing football. I did good. Get ready, baby."

My mask would use his gold and silver colors to attract unsuspecting females. He would act cool and calm and use a lot of flattery to lower the natural defense systems of the target. All through this, he would hide his true self from view as his own natural protection.

My mask would lure his target in with promises and bribery. Then he would use his targets and their weaknesses to his own advantage. And when they become suspicious of his actions, he let his true self be known and morally crushed the target until they were so full of pity and guilt that they didn't want to live anymore.

I am hurting the targets beyond repair. They will never be the same persons they were before they met me. By putting them in this situation, I am becoming no better than a rapist, or even a murderer. It takes a long time to work things out for yourself and not be a perpetrator, but it can be overcome, and I can have healthy relationships for the first time in my life.

I hurt myself by not knowing how to talk to girls. It lowers my self-esteem and I don't want to be around other people. I just take what I want, no matter what. It hurts the other person because she was taken advantage of. So she feels low and worth nothing.

It's not honest. You're lying to other people. You're repeating patterns of pain. They did it to me, I'll do it to them. It's not right but it's what I do.

You hurt yourself because you will become dependent on using the mask. You

hurt the other person because you use them. After awhile, the only way you can relate to other people is by using the mask. You will also lower other people's self-esteem. The other person may not trust anyone anymore.

Healthy Boundaries
for Healthy Relationships

Teens Can become less vulnerable to emotional grooming by learning how to set healthy boundaries for themselves and to respect others' boundaries as well. This chapter defines what healthy boundaries are, teaches how to set and maintain appropriate boundaries, and gives suggestions on how to spot boundary problems in ourselves and others.

What Are Boundaries?

There's a certain healthy physical and emotional distance that we keep between ourselves and others. This distance is often referred to as our "boundaries." Boundaries are the limits we have set for relationships. Boundaries define where one individual ends and where someone else begins. They help us to recognize what is and what is **not** your responsibility in relationships.

Imagine a series of invisible circles around your physical and emotional self. These circles determine how close you will let people get to you. These circles represent the various kinds of boundaries we all have.

Boundaries help determine how much we will share with others and how open or emotionally and physically close we are with all the various people in our life.

Boundaries work in two ways: They let people in, and they keep people out. Boundaries protect thoughts, feelings, the body, and behavior. They help tell us what's right or wrong. Setting and maintaining healthy boundaries can help us to protect and take responsibility for ourselves, and can even help us gain respect and show respect for others.

There are two types of boundaries:

External – External boundaries protect the body, keeping it safe and healthy. External boundaries have two components – physical and sexual. Physical boundaries protect the body and sexual boundaries protect sexual body parts and our sexuality.

Internal – Internal boundaries protect thoughts and emotions. Internal boundaries have two components – emotional and spiritual. Emotional boundaries help protect our feelings, and spiritual boundaries help protect the deepest part of who we are – our sense of hope, trust, mystery, security, and sense of spirituality.

Learning Our Boundaries

We begin learning about and setting boundaries at an early age. Parents help teach us right from wrong, as well as how and who to be physically and emotionally close to. When children are young, parents usually have all kinds of rules, like "Look both ways before crossing the street" and "Don't talk to strangers." Both of these rules are also boundaries, designed to help children protect their physical, emotional, sexual, and spiritual selves.

As children grow older and begin to develop more and more relationships outside the family, they begin to put what they've learned about boundaries into practice. Think about emotional boundaries for a moment. In your family, you probably learned to trust your parents and siblings enough to tell them your personal thoughts and feelings. As we grow older, most people continue to share their private thoughts and feelings only with family and best friends.

People with healthy boundaries are selective about who they allow inside their closest emotional and physical boundaries. They know that most relationships, like those with casual acquaintances or co-workers, are not as personal and therefore it is not wise to share personal thoughts, feelings, or experiences within such relationships. Not

enough trust has been established. Casual acquaintances should talk about "light" and non-personal topics like the weather, sports, movies, schoolwork, or current events. People with healthy boundaries would never consider giving personal information to a stranger. They learned long ago that "Don't talk to strangers" was a good boundary designed to protect them. A teen or young adult may occasionally talk to strangers, but only about topics such as the time, sports, weather or directions – never about anything personal.

As an example of physical boundaries, think about riding in an elevator alone. You have all that space to yourself and you can move around as you please. Gradually, other people get on the elevator. You're not as comfortable as when you were alone. More people get on the elevator; someone steps on your foot, you feel scrunched in a corner. You smell someone's breath or body odor. You feel uneasy because other people have entered the space where you once felt comfortable. They are just too close. You feel crowded and uneasy. They have crossed some of your physical boundaries.

For most Americans, a comfortable physical boundary with strangers is having an arm's length distance from that person. In other countries or cultures, the physical distance, or comfort zone, with strangers may be different. Physical boundaries, or comfort zones, change depending on the relationship and may also change over time as the relationship changes. Think about teens going on a first date. They are only casual acquaintances at this point. They should not feel comfortable holding hands yet. But after several dates, they may trust each other enough to hold hands, slow dance, or even hug.

People with healthy boundaries are:

- Secure with themselves.

- Don't let others intrude on them.

- Have a clear sense of their own views, values, and priorities.

- Are confident.

- Can protect themselves without shutting themselves off from others.

- Know how to stand up for themselves at appropriate times.

- Are able to enter into relationships without losing their own identity.

- Are able to identify safe and appropriate people.

Crossing Boundaries

In the elevator example, the people were strangers. Had they been your friends, you may not have felt as uncomfortable. But the same uncomfortable feeling of having boundaries "crossed" can occur in friendships and other close relationships, too. Friends and even family members can violate boundaries. When friends or family violate trust, they also violate boundaries.

Some boundary violations include:

- Interrupting a conversation

- Taking personal possessions without the owner's permission

- Teasing or making fun of others

- Asking very personal questions

- Gossiping about others

- Touching someone's body without his or her permission

- Revealing private information about yourself or others

- Constantly hanging around someone else or invading his or her "private space"

- Using offensive, vulgar, or sexually explicit language in others' presence

- Forcing someone into doing something sexual

- Physically hurting someone

So what should we do when someone crosses or violates our boundaries? Think of a soccer or basketball game. What happens when the ball goes out of bounds? The game stops for a short time. The team and the coaches may even meet to decide what to do next. It's a lot like that in life, too. When someone crosses one of our boundaries, whether it be a stranger, friend or family member, we need to step back from the situation and decide what to do next. It may help to talk to someone else we trust about what happened as well as how we feel. We can ask for help deciding what to do next.

In most cases, it's important to tell the person who violated our boundary what he or she did and how it was hurtful. Usually, an apology from the boundary crosser can go a long way toward rebuilding trust and rebuilding the relationship. Some boundary violations, however, are serious enough that we should never let that person get emotionally, physically, sexually, or spiritually close to us again.

Boundary Problems

Appropriate boundaries protect a person's physical, sexual, emotional, and spiritual self. But when appropriate boundaries aren't set, it can create a dangerous situation where a youth could get hurt or end up hurting someone else.

There are two kinds of boundary problems. Boundaries can be too closed (never sharing personal thoughts and emotions with others), or boundaries can be too open (indiscriminately sharing private thoughts, feelings or experiences with others we don't know well). Here are some signs of each kind of boundary problem.

Signs that boundaries are too open:

- Can't say "no"

- Shares too much personal information

- Takes responsibility for other's feelings

- Allows abuse

- Reveals personal thoughts, feelings, or experiences to acquaintances or strangers

- Believes he or she deserves bad treatment

- Can't see flaws in others

- Does anything to avoid conflict

- Engages in public displays of affection

- Wears revealing or seductive clothing (includes sagging pants)

- Has sexual encounters with acquaintances or strangers

- Stands or sits too close to others

- Makes sexual comments, jokes, or noises in public

- Trusts strangers

- Believes everything he or she hears

Signs that boundaries are too closed:

- Usually says "no" to requests that might require him or her to get close to someone

- Shares little or no personal information

- Is unable to identify own wants, needs, and feelings

- Doesn't have any friends

- Doesn't let adults help

- Never asks for help, even when needed

- Refuses to let trustworthy adults appropriately touch him or her (handshakes, pats on the back)

Boundary Problems in Friendship or Dating

How does a teen know if a relationship has unhealthy boundaries? A careful reading and discussion of the topics in the *Unmasking Sexual Con Games* Teen's Guide should give youth a pretty good idea of what an unhealthy relationship looks like and sounds like. They should be better at recognizing the nine grooming tactics and the emotional grooming process. The following questions can help them take a closer look at their friendships and dating relationships. Tell teens to be honest as they answer these questions. These questions may help point out unhealthy qualities in some of their relationships.

1. Does this person try to tell me what to do, how to dress, or who to hang out with?

2. Do I spend most of my time worrying about this relationship?

3. Does it seem that this person purposefully tries to make me feel jealous or insecure?

4. Does it seem that I do all the giving and my friend does all the taking?

5. Does my friend put unrealistic demands on me? What demands?

6. Does my friend ignore me or attempt to control me when others are around? What usually happens?

7. Does it seem like this friend is always trying to change me? How?

8. Does my friend purposefully do things to hurt me emotionally or physically? What?

9. Do other people tell me that my friend talks behind my back? About what?

10. Do I get into trouble when I do what my friend says? How?

11. Do I feel ashamed, guilty, or afraid after talking or being with this person?

12. Have I quit doing things that I used to enjoy since I've become involved with this person? What? Why?

13. Does this person ever threaten or intimidate me?

14. Has this person ever given me a gift and expected sexual contact in return?

A "yes" to any of these questions points to an unhealthy characteristic in a friendship. The more "yes" answers a teen has, the more unhealthy qualities the friendship has.

Teens should take some time to figure out if they can correct what's going wrong in the relationship (or if it's worth it). A lot of "no" answers indicate a healthy friendship. Teens should think about what they could do to make it even better.

If a teen has been used or abused in a relationship, there are a number of steps he or she can take. They include the following:

Tell someone who can help. Talk to someone you trust – a parent, a professional counselor, teacher, or other adult who will listen and offer help. Call a local crisis line or the toll-free Girls and Boys Town Hotline at 1-800-448-3000. Counselors are on call day and night to help with your problems.

Understand that change is possible. You're not weird or crazy. What happened was not your fault; someone took advantage of you. It's time to begin a new life that's free from unhealthy relationships.

Be honest. Admit that something bad happened to you. Don't make excuses for yourself or the person who used you. Don't hide the secret anymore. The pain will never stop if you don't do something about it. Let the pain end so the healing can begin.

Name, claim, and tame your feelings. You may be fearful, anxious, depressed, or just plain angry. All these feelings are normal. Name what you are feeling; expect some strong emotions. But don't keep your feelings bottled up inside. Talk to a counselor. Ask for ideas on how to handle feelings appropriately. Read books on how to handle negative or strong emotions. If you're depressed, ask for help; if you're angry, learn how to manage your anger, etc. Don't just feel bad; do something about it!

Learn to recognize the kinds of people and situations that can get you in trouble. Do some problem solving to find ways to avoid or get away from abusive people and negative environments. Try the P-O-P method of solving problems:

P – Identify the **problem** situation.

O – List various **options** for handling the situation and the advantages and disadvantages of each.

P – Decide on a **plan** to handle the problem by choosing one of the options to put into action. Assess the success of your plan and decide if anything else needs to be done.

Learn how to create and maintain healthy boundaries. Read all you can about healthy boundaries and friendship. Observe people who have good boundaries and healthy friendships. Take notice of what makes good relationships grow. Then put into practice what you've learned.

Learn healthy responses to stress. Things may worry you; people may upset you. Get involved in positive activities. Join a support group. Exercise. Doing kind and helpful things for others will help you avoid getting bogged down in self-pity.

Setting Appropriate Boundaries

There are many ways to set and maintain appropriate boundaries. The following tips can help youth set good boundaries:

■ Identify teens and adults you can trust and build relationships with them.

■ Avoid people who are selfish, disrespectful, manipulative, or abusive. Such people will likely disrespect you and your boundaries.

■ Spend time with people who do well in school and at home, who are liked and respected by many people. Such people are more likely to have good boundaries themselves and will be more likely to respect your boundaries too.

■ Learn to say "no" when you're being pressured to do something wrong. Anyone who pressures or invites you to do something wrong doesn't respect you or your boundaries.

■ Trust your sense of safety or danger. These are good indicators of right and wrong. If someone or something seems dangerous or threatening, stay away!

■ Learn how to think through and solve problems before reacting. Problem solving and critical thinking skills can help you maintain your boundaries and respect others.

■ Think about times when your personal boundaries were violated. Who was involved? What was the situation? Think of a better way to handle boundary violations in the future.

■ Speak up when someone or something bothers you. Talk to adults you can trust.

■ Set limits about where you will go, what you will do, and how long you will be there. Having and sticking to a plan helps you keep and respect boundaries.

■ Find ways to tell (or show) others what your personal boundaries are.

Rules for Good Boundaries

Different kinds of relationships have different kinds of boundaries. Physical, emotional, sexual, and spiritual boundaries with parents and siblings look different than the boundaries we have with friends. The boundaries we have with a stranger would be different than the boundaries we have with classmates or co-workers. Below are some good questions for teens to ask themselves as a relationship or friendship is developing. These are general rules to follow that can help youth establish and maintain good boundaries in all their relationships. Honestly reflecting on each of these areas can help teens make wise decisions about who they decide to become friends with or date.

Length of time – How long have you known this person? How can knowing someone longer be beneficial to you? How long is long enough before a stranger becomes a friend? How do you decide?

Knowledge about the other person – What, and how much, do you really know about this person? Some important things to know about someone you are considering dating are:

■ How does this person react when given "no" for an answer?

■ How does this person handle frustrations and disappointments?

■ How does he or she express anger?

■ How does this person treat his or her parents?

■ How does this person speak about and treat the other gender?

How can this knowledge help you make good choices in a relationship?

Sharing activities – How many different kinds of activities have you shared together with this person? What are they? How have these experiences helped you get to know the other person better?

Amount of self-disclosure – How much personal information have you shared? How much has the other person shared? Are you comfortable with the sharing? Why or why not? Is the amount of sharing equal between the two of you?

Number of different experiences – What has this person experienced in life? How has it affected him or her? What can this person's experiences tell you about him or her?

Role appropriate – We all have certain roles in life. Some roles are incompatible for dating or friendship relationships. Teachers don't date students; doctors don't date patients, etc. What role does this person have in your life?

Age appropriate – As adolescents, friendships or dating relationships with those two or more years older or younger than us can be harmful. What is the age difference between you? If it is greater than two years, how could this be harmful?

Level of reciprocal trust – Can you trust this person? How do you know? Are you worthy of his or her trust? Why? How do you know when someone is trustworthy? What happens when trust is broken?

Length of Time

When developing new relationships, teens need to remember that time is on their side! Really getting to know someone takes time. It doesn't happen overnight. The more we know about someone, the better judgments we can make about how close to allow them. Youth should never rush into a relationship or allow someone to rush them. Teens should build a relationship gradually. If it is good, it will last.

Knowledge about the Other Person

Getting to know someone involves spending "real" time together, (not just "virtual time" chatting on the computer), as well as talking about many things – learning about his or her family, likes and dislikes, hopes and dreams for the future, past experiences, etc. When considering a close relationship with someone, there are some really important things youth should know including: How does this person react when hearing "no" for an answer? How does he or she treat parents? How does he or she speak about the opposite gender when with friends? How does the person handle frustrations and anger? We can learn such important information not only by discussing these issues but also by observing how he or she interacts with others. This is why group dating can be helpful. It allows youth to see the other person interact with a variety of people. If the person is a player, he or she won't be able to hide it for long. The more teens know, the better their decisions can be.

Amount of Self-Disclosure and Trust

How much personal information should be shared with someone we are just getting to know? The best rule of thumb is to share a small bit of personal information, something we wouldn't really mind if others found out about. Then see what happens. If he or she respects our boundaries, and us, then personal information won't become public news. But if personal information is given to others, it's a sure sign that this person is not trustworthy.

How do we know if someone is really trustworthy? Real trust is built; it takes time. It is something we prove through our actions, not just something we say with words. A trustworthy person is someone who keeps his or her promises, who is there in good times and in bad, and who tells the truth even when it's hard.

Trust is hard earned but easily broken. Sometimes even our family and closest friends will break our trust and violate our boundaries. When that happens, an apology with appropriate amends can go a long way toward rebuilding trust and repairing the relationship.

Role and Age Appropriate

We all have certain roles in life. Some roles are incompatible for dating or even friendship relationships. Teachers should not date or seek students out as friends; doctors should not date patients; coaches should not date or seek out the athletes they coach as friends, etc. Certain relationships are designed to be dependent, where one person has more knowledge, power, or status than the other. Because of their dependent nature, these types of relationships are not conducive to dating or friendship.

Friendships or dating relationships with those two or more years older or younger than an adolescent can be harmful. Consider the differences between the life experiences of someone in seventh grade and someone in twelfth grade. A two-or-more year age difference in high school dating relationships may lead not only to minor misunderstandings but major unrealistic or harmful expectations in relationships as well.

Looking for Balance

A friendship or a dating relationship should always involve give and take from both people. That doesn't mean teens need to keep a scorecard of what they and their friends do for one another, but it is a good idea to see if there is a healthy balance there. They should evaluate relationships and try to find that balance. No person should be in control or do all of the taking. In other words, teens and their friends or dating partners should have similar expectations for relationships.

It's also good for youth to keep in mind that friendship and dating are just one portion of life. Spending too much time thinking about one relationship takes away from all of the other important things they should be concentrating on. Teens need to take care of their responsibilities to family, school, church, and community. Friends should respect their choice to do so.

Youth should realize that friendships and dating relationships will change; some will change for the better, some for the worse. They should be encouraged to learn how to adjust to these changes. They can strive to be flexible and understanding of others while sticking with the things they know are right.

Ask teens to look at past relationships that were positive and make a list of the things that made those relationships healthy. They should identify any positive changes friends have helped them make and then name the things they do to help make positive changes in others.

It may also help teens to examine relationships that didn't work out. Although relationships are a two-way street, they can try to figure out what part they played in making each relationship end up the way it did. Encourage them to remember what they learned from past relationships so that they can avoid those mistakes in the future.

Getting Started: Implementing the Curriculum

Before implementing the *Unmasking Sexual Con Games* curriculum, there is some important groundwork to be done. The very content of this curriculum demands that rules of conduct, classroom climate, communication, and teacher-student as well as student-student relationships need to be considered. This chapter will help you prepare to set up a classroom that encourages respect and fosters learning.

Modeling Good Social Skills

Being a good teacher involves more than preparing lessons, classroom set-up, and grading papers. Good teachers want their students to learn not only the content presented but also how to get along with others. A student's success is not only marked by good grades but also by good social skills. Teachers know that students who want to be successful both in and outside the classroom will need to master skills that will enable them to have appropriate and healthy relationships – with peers and with adults. And good teachers know that one of the most effective ways to teach good social skills and help youth create and maintain healthy relationships is to model appropriate social skills and build good relationships with students and colleagues.

Ways to model and build good relationships:

- Really listen to the youth – individually and as a group.

- Show genuine interest in their lives and stories.

- Be encouraging and supportive.

- Pay attention to discover their gifts and talents.

- Look for something they do well and affirm it.

- Give sincere compliments.

- Say "thanks" for their time, their help, their ideas, their enthusiasm, and so forth.

- Use your sense of humor – but never be sarcastic.

- Do not speak ill of someone; those who hear will wonder what you say about them.

- Practice and enforce the Golden Rule.

Some youth, and especially those who have been sexually used or abused, have had difficulty building healthy relationships and have had their boundaries crossed and broken. These youth may have low self-esteem and underdeveloped social skills and are prime candidates for a sexual con artist. Many of these youth also have problems developing relationships with adults, especially parents, teachers, and employers. Some helpful hints to keep in mind when working with teens who have had boundary issues are:

- Use a calm, pleasant voice tone. Youth respond better to an adult who isn't harsh or punishing.

- Take time to listen and understand. Sometimes, adults tend to view a problem as minor when the problem is a source of true pain for a young person.

- Use examples to help youth learn acceptable social skills. Explain how to react or what to do in a given situation.

- Give reasons why a youth should or shouldn't behave in a certain way. Youth need to see the link between behavior and outcomes.

- Be direct and honest. Some topics – even those that may be sensitive in nature – are best addressed in an open, factual manner.

- Set (and adhere to) clear rules and expectations. Don't hesitate to correct inappropriate behaviors and set reasonable limits.

Setting Classroom Boundaries

Only by having positive relationships with your students can you begin to teach them the skills they need in order to avoid or escape the sexual con artist. It is our job to educate our youth about healthy as well as harmful relationships. Therefore, we must be living examples of how to create healthy relationships.

Another very important component of creating and maintaining good relationships is setting and maintaining appropriate boundaries for the youth in your class. Setting and maintaining boundaries helps create a positive and safe learning environment.

Some examples of boundaries appropriate for the classroom are:

- One person speaks at a time.

- Keep your hands to yourself.

- Be on time.

- Use appropriate language. No cussing or swear words.

- Show respect for others by not putting them down.

The most effective time to set boundaries is at the beginning of the year, or at the first session of your planned meetings. Once established, list and post these boundaries so they can be referred to often. It can be helpful to remind youth of these boundaries:

- After holiday or vacation time

- Before an upcoming event – to proactively teach specific boundaries

- After a problem has occurred – in order to correct inappropriate behavior and remind them of boundaries and why we follow them

The principal, program director, and teachers, along with parents and adults from your community, should give specific input as to what behaviors are expected and appropriate for youth. Along with clarifying what is expected from youth, these adults should also establish guidelines for what to do when boundaries are broken. It may be helpful to include selected youth leaders from your school or organization to be a part of this initial conversation. These youth may be able to provide insights and situational examples that can help determine more clear, fair, and necessary recommendations.

After you have clear ideas and direction from adults and parents, the next step is to meet with the youth themselves. Try the following activity to help youth name, clarify, and take ownership of specific boundaries they will need to follow to create and maintain a positive environment.

Boundary-Setting Activity with Youth

STEP ONE: Ask youth to brainstorm and list their responses to these two questions:

- What damages or destroys relationships?

- What builds or nourishes relationships?

Encourage youth to name specific actions and attitudes that fit into each list. (Damages – rumors, cheating, two-faced behavior, talking behind one's back. Nourishes – respect, spending time, listening, etc.) Allow students plenty of time to add to the list. Make sure adults wait to add to either list until youth have finished.

STEP TWO: After completing the lists, ask: *"What do you notice about these lists?"*

Again, allow plenty of time for their responses. Hopefully, they will notice that the contents of lists are usually opposites of one another. They may also notice that contents of these lists are how we want to be treated or don't want to be treated by others – the Golden Rule.

STEP THREE: Next, explain to the students: *"The purpose of this activity was to help us begin to think about the specific boundaries we need to keep in order to create an environment where relationships are nourished, not damaged. You have just listed how you want and don't want to be treated by others. Let's condense these two lists into one list of the Ten Most Important Boundaries/Rules for Behavior."* Before naming boundaries, offer youth these helpful suggestions:

1. Keep it simple. State the boundary clearly and concisely.

   "One person speaks at a time."

   "Disagree appropriately."

2. State it positively. Tell them what they should do and how to do it. "Thou SHALL…" instead of "Thou shall NOT…"

   "Be in the classroom, at your desk, before the bell rings."

3. Stick to the "Golden Rule." Treat others the way you would like to be treated – with the kind of respect you desire and each person deserves.

When the students are finished listing their ideas, add any other boundaries you deem necessary.

STEP FOUR: Create and post your new list of boundaries. Send copies home to parents to read and discuss. Refer to the list often!

STEP FIVE: Make sure to let youth know that these boundaries are **expectations.** If they break a boundary, let them know that there will be consistent consequences and what those consequences will be. Be sure to consult with your principal or program director for exact procedures regarding consequences. It is most important that the youth know that:

■ There are specific boundaries for behaviors that **everyone** is expected to follow.

■ Maintaining these boundaries will help make this an environment where all are safe and welcomed.

■ There are pre-established and appropriate consequences for breaking boundaries. (More on how to set and enforce consequences later.)

■ The teacher or another designated adult will address any broken boundaries in a fair and dignified way. (More on this in the next section.)

Be sure to explain why it is important for all of us to maintain appropriate and healthy boundaries.

"They help us know how to treat one another and how we can expect to be treated."

"Following these rules will help us all learn to show respect to others."

"Maintaining boundaries helps us create good relationships."

Methods for Teaching to and Maintaining Boundaries

Along with naming boundaries, you also need ways to maintain and reinforce boundaries with youth. Here are three tried and true methods from the youth care specialists at Girls and Boys Town:

Proactive Teaching

Set youth up for success by specifically naming and briefly explaining the boundaries/expected behaviors **before** each event or activity. A little preventive teaching goes a long way in stopping behaviors before they get started.

The steps to Proactive Teaching are:

1. **Describe the behaviors that are appropriate and/or expected for this event or activity.**

2. **Give a reason.**

3. **Practice the behavior. (optional)**

EXAMPLE: In a Girls Support Group, gossiping and complaining can quickly ruin a good discussion. Use Proactive Teaching to remind the girls:

1. *"When describing a problem or situation, please do not use any names. Stick to*

talking only about yourself and your feelings. No blaming or complaining."

2. *"It's important to do this for many reasons: Because people don't want to be talked about behind their backs; it is not fair to discuss someone who is not present; we are about solving problems, not laying blame or complaining."*

It's amazing how these simple boundaries can prevent potentially serious problems and enable the girls to speak more freely, trust one another more, and resolve conflicts in a more responsible fashion!

Effective Praise

One of the best ways to help youth do the right thing is to "catch them doing the right thing." We all need reassurance that we're doing what we are supposed to. We all like to receive praise and compliments. A great way to ensure that a positive behavior is repeated is to recognize it with praise. Tell youth what they're doing right, when they're doing a good job, and be sure to name exactly what it is that they are doing a good job of. Then they'll know exactly what to do right the next time!

The steps to Effective Praise are:

1. **Show your approval.** Smile, speak a word of praise or thanks, or give a pat on the back.

2. **Describe the positive.** Name it specifically: *"Alan, thanks for waiting for Juana to finish speaking before stating your point."* or, *"Allison, I really appreciated your note to let me know that you'd be late for the planning meeting!"*

3. **Give a reason.** Tell them why what they did was good, important, or helpful. To Alan: *"Waiting for someone to finish speaking before you speak is a great way to show respect and to show that you are really listening!"* To Allison: *"Your note helped me use that extra time wisely instead of worrying and waiting."*

Corrective Teaching

Boundary breaking is bound to happen. We all cross a boundary now and then, sometimes by accident and sometimes on purpose. Our task as adults is to provide consistent management of boundaries, whether kept or broken. It is important to know, **in advance,** what to do when boundaries or rules are broken. Corrective Teaching, coupled with appropriate consequences, is a most effective method for transforming a broken boundary into a teachable moment.

The steps to Corrective Teaching are:

1. **Stop the problem behavior.** As soon as you notice a broken boundary, address it. Sometimes just moving closer to the problem behavior – moving to sit next to the two whispering teens or catching the eye of those involved – can stop the problem. Other times a prompt, spoken in a calm and descriptive manner, can help youth get back on track: *"Remember, no talking during this activity."*

2. **Give a consequence.** Sometimes it is enough to have an adult leader sit next to a student or to receive a quick corrective prompt from the teacher. Other times, a more substantial consequence is needed.

3. **Describe the positive behavior the youth should do.** Now that the youth knows what **not to do,** let him or her know what **to do:** *"Instead of whispering to Shannon, please give your quiet attention to our guest speaker."*

4. **Give youth a chance to engage in positive behavior.** Walk away but keep an eye out for appropriate behavior. Watch for, and praise any steps in the right direction.

Guidelines for Consequences

- Consequences should be established by adults and communicated to youth and parents in advance! Don't wait for a situation to arise before deciding what the consequence will be. It is best to have predetermined consequences that are well communicated to all before any boundaries are broken. Consequences decided on the spur of the moment can too easily become punishing, vengeful, or too drastic.

- Consequences should never be degrading or humiliating. They should be opportunities for learning responsibility and respect.

- Consequences should be given fairly and consistently. All youth should be held accountable for maintaining these boundaries. Don't play favorites or let youth talk their way out of owning up to the misbehavior.

- Corrective Teaching and administering consequences should be done one-to-one whenever possible, even if it means taking a youth aside for a moment. If Corrective Teaching does need to happen in front of others, make sure other youth are busy with another task before calmly and quietly approaching the student who needs correction. Use a low voice and be at eye level with the youth. Shouting a correction across the room, shaking your fist, wagging your finger, or making sarcastic comments may only cause the youth to become more angry or embarrassed and you then run the risk of escalating the problem rather than correcting it.

- Ask for help from parents and other adults. Sometimes the presence of other adults helps youth stay on track. These "extra" adults could be used as "time-out" folks – someone to send a youth to be with when the misbehavior causes the youth to be removed from the large group activity. These "time-out" folks are not meant to be disciplinarians, but rather an option for a youth who may need some extra one-on-one time with an adult to calm down or work through a problem.

Addressing and correcting any problems promptly and without much disruption sends a powerful message to the whole group. It lets them know that you are watching out for them, that you care about how they treat one another, and that you keep your word. They need to see that you will be firm, yet gentle, in safeguarding their boundaries. Your actions speak much louder than words in these instances.

Always remember the Golden Rule when correcting behaviors: **Treat youth as you would want to be treated.** Put yourself in that teen's place. Show genuine empathy and understanding rather than anger or dominance.

Top Ten Boundaries for Youth Group Activities

Here are some time-tested, success-inspiring, "catch them being good" boundaries that address areas of behavior that are common to most youth-oriented gatherings.

1. **One person speaks at a time.** Whether in small or large group discussions, this is an ever-present opportunity to show respect and to really listen to what everyone has to say.

2. **Disagree appropriately.** This is a very important skill to teach, model, role-play, and use. Disagreeing appropriately allows opinions to be voiced without aggression or disrespect. It teaches us how to accept and allow others to be different. It can defuse tense situations. (See the next section for this skill and others.)

3. **No putdowns are allowed.** Show respect to others by refraining from making value judgments about them: "You may not use words like 'stupid,' 'dumb,' 'ugly,' 'gross,' or other judgmental, negative words to describe people or their thoughts. Say 'please be quiet' instead of 'shut up.' No teasing, even if only in fun."

4. **Say whatever you want as long as it is appropriate.** What is said should be on the topic and not contain any obscene or offensive language.

5. **What is said here, stays here.** This boundary helps create trust, safety, and a sense of community. The exception to this rule is when an adult needs to seek help for a teen in danger. When anyone makes any reference to doing something harmful or illegal to themselves or someone else, we need to speak up and seek help. Do not keep this information to yourself.

6. **Self-disclose appropriately.** Personal dumping, public confessions, blaming or complaining are never allowed. If this does happen, the teacher should politely interrupt and steer the conversation back on track.

7. **Practice good listening skills.** Looking at the person who is speaking, concentrating on what is being said, etc., all show respect for others.

8. **Observe school/organizational rules about public displays of affection (PDAs).** It is important to state this clearly. Such displays can cause serious problems among youth groups. Some recommended PDA rules: "Refrain from hand holding, kissing, cuddling, or any other form of exclusive affection at school/youth group activities. Ask permission before giving a hug – especially to newcomers."

9. **Ask for help.** Youth should be encouraged to seek assistance from adults or youth leaders whenever they need it.

10. **Participate.** "You get out of class what you put into class. So get into it!"

Setting clear rules and expectations early helps prevent problems that can arise when young people engage in any kind of discussion or activity, especially when the topic involves sex, dating, and relationships. Firm, but reasonable, guidelines help each young person learn in an environment that is comfortable, open, and appropriate.

Keep the following suggestions in mind when establishing your guidelines. Remember to state any rules in terms that young people clearly understand.

1. **Monitor youth group activities.** Have a "healthy" paranoia. Make sure youth are where they are supposed to be and doing what they are supposed to be doing. Keeping a watchful eye on their behavior also allows you opportunities to praise them for following rules and to teach alternative behaviors when necessary.

2. **Teach youth how to respond to inappropriate sexual advances.**

3. **Define appropriate and inappropriate classroom behavior.** Let the youth know what your tolerances are and what will be reported to their parents or guardians.

4. **Teach youth how to report inappropriate behavior.**

5. **Encourage participation.** Discourage any negative behaviors, such as putdowns, name-calling, or inappropriate facial expressions.

6. **Have specific rules regarding what can and can't be talked about in class.** Remember that you are first and foremost their teacher, not their friend or counselor.

7. **Spend time listening to and communicating with your youth.** Topics such as sex, dating, and relationships are confusing and, sometimes, frightening to them.

8. **Present balanced and accurate information on the wide-ranging effects of premarital sexual activity** – physical, social, intellectual, emotional, moral, spiritual, legal.

9. **Be a good role model.** Avoid all sexual innuendoes. You may be engaging in behavior that can be misunderstood by your students. Such behavior may even be stimulating to some youth. Realize that for a few youth, even a pat on the back can be misunderstood.

Boundaries for One-to-Ones with Teens

When a teen asks to talk to you privately, there are some important boundaries to make known:

1. Some things cannot be kept secret. Let teens know that if they share thoughts of hurting themselves or someone else, or reveal involvement in illegal, sexual, or abusive activity, that you have a moral and sometimes legal obligation to tell someone else who can help them. In these serious circumstances, a teen's physical and emotional life is at stake. We must let youth know that we value their life above all else, even above their possible anger at "telling" on them.

2. Meet in an open space where you can be seen, but not overheard, by others. If meeting in an office, keep the door

open, or use only an office with uncovered windows. This can prevent any allegations of misconduct and provide you both with the security of knowing others are around.

3. Remind youth that you are not a trained counselor, but that you can point them in the right direction. Have referral sources available with names and phone numbers of professionals who can help.

Skills That Build Boundaries

What is a skill? It is a step-by-step approach, a "how to" method of learning proper behaviors. There are all kinds of skills – academic skills, study skills, communication skills, and social skills – to name a few. Learning more about and practicing social skills and communication skills can help youth learn how to relate to one another and to adults in a more appropriate and healthy manner. Some important social skills include:

■ How to disagree appropriately

■ How to accept criticism

■ How to give and receive compliments

■ How to ask for help

■ How to share personal experiences

■ How to express empathy and understanding of others

■ How to follow rules

■ How to apologize and accept apologies

Steps to these social skills are listed at the end of this chapter.

Teaching youth skills can help them be more successful when faced with awkward, difficult, and even dangerous situations. Teaching skills to youth helps them be prepared, know what to expect, and how to behave in a variety of situations. Skills can help teens learn how to:

Be assertive. Teens can learn how to get their ideas and feelings across without making matters worse. If they are in a situation that can be harmful to them, they have to learn and practice how to say "No."

Talk to a trusted adult. Teens can learn how to name and own their own thoughts and feelings without blaming others and without revealing too much.

Know personal boundaries. Teens can learn what emotional, physical, sexual, and spiritual boundaries are as well as how to set, protect, and respect such boundaries.

Ask for help. Youth often feel powerless and at the mercy of the adults in their lives. Skills can enable them to share feelings appropriately with the appropriate person.

Solve problems. Teens can learn how to look at a variety of options before reaching a decision. Teens are more likely to use the portion of their brain that is dominated by emotions. They need to learn how to think critically. Skills can help teens do just that.

Deal with peer pressure. Teens can learn how to recognize whether something is right or wrong, helpful or harmful. Learning and practicing skills can enable teens to learn how to avoid and get out of negative situations.

Be a good friend. Teens can learn what true friendship entails and the skills necessary to create and maintain friendships.

Set goals. Teens can learn how to set achievable goals and how to reach them.

Important Social Skills

How to Disagree Appropriately

1. Look at the person.

2. Use a pleasant voice.

3. Say, *"I understand how you feel."*

4. Tell why you feel differently.

5. Give a reason.

6. Listen to the other person.

How to Accept Criticism

1. Look at the person.

2. Say, *"Okay."*

3. Don't argue.

How to Give Compliments

1. Look at the person.

2. Speak with a clear, enthusiastic voice.

3. Praise the person's behavior. Tell him or her exactly what you like.

4. Use words such as *"That's great,"* *"Wonderful,"* or *"That was awesome."*

5. Give the other person time to respond to your compliment.

How to Accept Compliments

1. Look at the person who is complimenting you.

2. Use a pleasant tone of voice.

3. Thank the person sincerely for the compliment. Say, *"Thanks for noticing"* or *"I appreciate that."*

4. Do not look away, mumble, or deny the compliment.

How to Ask for Help

1. Get the person's attention without interrupting. Wait to be acknowledged.

2. Look at the person.

3. Use a pleasant tone of voice.

4. Ask for help using words such as *"Please," "Would you be able to," "What can I,"* or *May I…"*

5. Listen to the person's answer.

6. Thank the person for his or her time.

How to Express Feelings Appropriately

1. Remain calm and relaxed.

2. Look at the person you are talking to.

3. Describe the feelings you are having.

4. Avoid using profanity or statements of blame.

5. Take responsibility for the feelings you are having.

6. Thank the person for listening.

How to Follow Instructions

1. Look at the person.

2. Say, "Okay."

3. Do the task immediately.

4. Check back.

How to Accept "No"

1. Look at the person.

2. Say, "Okay."

3. Calmly ask for a reason if you really don't understand.

4. If you disagree, bring it up later.

How to Express Empathy and Understanding of Others

1. Listen closely to the other person's words. Try to understand what he or she is feeling.

2. Express empathy by saying, *"I understand..."*

3. Demonstrate concern through words and actions.

4. Reflect back the other person's words by saying, *"It seems like you are saying..."*

5. Offer any help you can.

How to Apologize

1. Look at the person.

2. Use a serious, sincere tone of voice. Don't pout.

3. Begin by saying, *"I wanted to apologize for"* or *"I'm sorry for..."*

4. Do not make excuses or give rationalizations.

How to Accept an Apology

1. Look at the person who is apologizing.

2. Listen to what he or she is saying.

3. Remain calm. Refrain from any sarcastic statements.

4. Thank the person for the apology. Say, *"Thanks for saying you're sorry"* or *"That's Okay."*

Additional social skills and their behavioral steps can be found in *Teaching Social Skills to Youth*, by Tom Dowd and Jeff Tierney, 1992, Boys Town Press, 1-800-282-6657.

Lesson Plans

Teachers in both classroom settings and youth group meeting formats have successfully implemented the following lesson plans. We suggest that you follow these as closely as possible within the context of your work with youth. Feel free to adapt the lesson plans to fit the emotional, intellectual, and age level of your youth, and the time frame within which you are presenting the material.

We have found that one very effective method for covering the material in the Teen's Guide is the tried and true Socratic method – students read the material, on their own or aloud together as a class, while the teacher facilitates comprehension by frequently stopping to ask or answer questions arising from the material. We also have discovered that this material works best when taught in same gender groups with a same gender teacher. Most young men and women seem more comfortable and receptive, ask more questions, and participate more in this type of setting. Same gender groups can not only help teens learn how to create healthy friendships with members of the same gender, but can also be a place to learn how to maintain good boundaries and a sense of modesty.

Below are a few helpful techniques when reading and discussing as a group.

■ Each youth should have a highlighter and should underline key passages as noted by the teacher.

■ Students should take turns reading aloud. For variety, have the current reader toss a foam ball to another student as a way to call on the next reader.

■ Stop after every paragraph or two and ask for questions or comments. The teacher should prepare discussion questions from the pages to be covered each session. Students can then discuss or write out their responses as an assignment.

■ The teacher should create notes, reviews, quizzes, and tests based on the content presented in the Teen's Guide.

session 1

Unmasking Sexual Con Games

OBJECTIVE: To explore the purpose and symbolism of masks in order to enable students to better understand the purpose of this course.

LEADER PREPARATION: Display a variety of masks around the room, such as Halloween masks, carnival masks, costume masks, or papier-mâché masks. (This session may take more than one class period to complete.)

STEP ONE: Allow students a few minutes to observe the various masks. Then discuss the following questions:

- What did you notice about the masks?

- Which was your favorite mask? Why?

- Which mask did you like the least? Why?

- What is the purpose of a mask?

- When or why might someone wear a mask?

STEP TWO: Summarize and make the following points for the group by saying something like:

"For the purpose of this course, we are going to discuss the kinds of masks people wear when they are trying to hide or keep something about themselves from being discovered. We are not talking about real masks that you can see, like a Halloween mask, a carnival mask, or even a circus clown's painted-on mask. We will be talking about 'masks' that are much harder to see – symbolic masks. This course is designed to help you learn how to identify the kind of masks some people put on in order to use or manipulate others. Their masks are worn to hide their true intention – to use you. Their masks may take the form of words, behaviors, or mind games – like trying to make you feel guilty or scared. But in the end, their manipulative words and behaviors are still a mask, a cover-up, and a con game, all designed to hide from you their true intentions – using and manipulating you."

STEP THREE: Give each student a copy of the Teen's Guide. Introduce and define two terms they will hear often throughout this course – "emotional grooming" and "emotional groomer."

Emotional grooming: When a person plays with someone else's emotions and attempts to gain control of that person, usually in order to coax the person into some kind of sexual relationship.

Emotional groomer: A person who tries to gain control of another person, usually in order to begin a manipulative sexual relationship. An emotional groomer is also known as a sexual con artist. Other names for emotional groomers include player, pimp, or perpetrator. (pages 2-7 in Teen's Guide).

Write these definitions on the board or display them on an overhead. Add to these definitions by stating:

"An emotional groomer wears 'masks' and plays con games. An emotional groomer wants to con or manipulate you in order to use you sexually. That's a sexual con game. This Teen's Guide is designed to help you understand what emotional grooming and sexual con games are and how to avoid them so that you can have healthy and happy relationships. This Teen's Guide will help you to 'unmask' the groomer's con games, or tricks, so that you can see and learn how to avoid the groomer's true intention, which is to use you."

STEP FOUR: Read and discuss Chapters 1 through 3, pages 1-25 in the Teen's Guide. Spend as much time as students need to read and discuss thoroughly. Remember to stop after every paragraph or two and ask for questions or comments from the group. You may also want to point out the sections or sentences you'd like them to highlight for future reference.

STEP FIVE: Direct students to answer the questions on the Emotional Grooming Worksheet for this session. These questions could be completed individually, in small groups, or even as a homework assignment.

STEP SIX: To summarize their learning, ask students to complete the following statements, aloud or in writing. If the questions are to be answered aloud, invite, but do not force, each student to respond.

1. Something I learned or realized today is:

2. One question I have is:

TEACHER NOTES: Read the entire Leader's Guide and Teen's Guide **before** teaching this course. Make sure you re-read the section you are going to cover with your class **before** class begins. Jot down helpful notes or questions in the margins of your Leader's Guide or your personal Teen's Guide.

Begin each new session with the youths' questions or important points from the last session.

If students are not asking questions, ask them the questions that you've jotted down in your Teen's Guide, or ask them for other examples that relate to the assignment.

Name_____

Emotional Grooming Worksheet

1. Define emotional grooming.

2. What is a sexual con game?

3. List some other names for an emotional groomer.

4. What are the two elements of the grooming process?

5. How does alcohol and drug use affect the grooming process?

6. What is a language con?

7. List four characteristics of a language con.

Emotional Grooming Tactics

OBJECTIVE: To enable each student to assess his or her own potential for "grooming" others or of being "groomed" and to learn the nine grooming tactics. (This session may take more than one class period to complete.

STEP ONE: Review the previous session by asking volunteers to name:

- Something they have learned so far.

- Something they still have a question about.

STEP TWO: Prepare to administer the relationship questionnaire by saying:

"Today we are going to begin class by completing a questionnaire. The questions are designed to help you assess the quality of current and past relationships. The purpose of answering these questions is to learn more about yourself and what you may need to change in order to have healthier relationships."

Before administering the questionnaire, you should:

- Distribute a copy of the blank answer sheet in this lesson plan to each student. Explain, that in order to protect their privacy, their names should **not** be written on the answer sheet.

- Continue explaining by saying, *"You will be the only one to see your answers. Mark your responses to the questions as I read them aloud. For each question, decide whether it is something that has been done to you or something you have done to others. Answer by circling yes, no, or sometimes in each column."*

- Also explain, "It is important for us to respect one another's privacy. Because this is very personal information no one should say his or her answers aloud and no one should look at anyone else's answers. I will not look at your answers, either. Please do not put your name or anything that could identify you on your answer sheet. After class you will throw away your answer sheet."

- Add, "If you do not understand a question, please raise your hand and I will explain it. After you have answered all the questions, I will explain how to determine your score."

STEP THREE: Begin administering the questionnaire. You may show the questions on an overhead transparency and/or read them aloud, one by one, to the class. Read each question slowly and clearly, pause, and then re-read the same question, as well as the possible responses, yes, no, or sometimes.

DO NOT reproduce the questionnaire to hand out as a worksheet. Papers that have both the questions and a student's answers can easily be lost or taken from a student, thereby compromising his or her privacy.

STEP FOUR: After completing the questionnaire, ask each student to tally the number of "yes" responses, the number of "no" responses, and the number of "sometimes" responses. Once everyone has completed their tallies, ask them to circle the numbers of any question marked with a "yes" or "sometimes" answer. Show the questionnaire again so that they can see the original questions.

Explain that each of the questions is designed to help them assess whether or not they are tolerating or perpetrating an unhealthy behavior. Point out that the specific unhealthy behaviors addressed in the questionnaire are:

- Questions 1-5 point to issues of sexual harassment.

- Questions 6-10 are all boundary violations.

- Questions 11-13 are all issues of sexual assault or rape.

- Questions 14-22 each deal with one or more grooming tactics.

- Questions 23-27 deal with ways in which sex can be misused.

Point out that each time they answered "yes" or "sometimes," it indicates some sort of inappropriate boundary and will point to an aspect of relationships where improvement is needed. The more of these that a student answered "Yes, I have done this to others" the more likely it is that he or she is engaging in grooming behavior.

Note that if they answered "no" to doing these things to others, but recognized that they allow others to behave toward them in any of these ways, then they most likely have been "groomed" and are vulnerable to being targeted again. Now would be a good time to set and maintain firmer and healthier boundaries!

STEP FIVE: Allow some time for discussion and clarification of the relationship questions.

Remind students to use appropriate language when they ask questions or participate in a discussion. Some youth may not know the correct terms or how to phrase a question appropriately, especially when it comes to matters of sexuality. Listen closely to their questions or comments, and ask for more information, if appropriate. Use your best judgment when deciding what is or is not appropriate for the group to discuss.

Discussions should be as general and objective as possible. **If a youth begins to disclose something too personal, ask the youth to stop and tell him or her that you will discuss this matter later in private.** If you do choose to talk with a youth privately, make sure that you are not totally alone. Meet someplace where you can talk without being overheard, but where you can still be seen by others. Do not meet behind a closed door. It is possible that lies, rumors, or innuendoes could develop. Adult leaders should not meet alone with youth of the opposite sex. Instead, have another adult of the same sex as the youth continue the conversation or be present while you meet with that youth.

Be sure that students discard their answer sheets before leaving the classroom.

STEP SIX: After discussion of the questionnaire is complete, direct students to open their Teen's Guide to Chapter 4, "The Nine Grooming Tactics," on page 33.

Introduce this chapter by saying: *"Remember that the purpose of the questionnaire was to help you recognize if you are tolerating or perpetrating any unhealthy behaviors in your relationships. In particular, questions 14-22 described some of the unhealthy and manipulative behaviors a groomer uses to con or coerce others. We are now going to spend some time reading about the nine grooming tactics so that you will become better able to recognize and avoid these unhealthy and manipulative behaviors that damage and destroy relationships."*

Read and discuss the chapter on emotional grooming tactics. Remember to stop after every tactic and ask for questions or comments from the group. You may also want to point out the paragraphs or sentences you'd like them to highlight for future reference.

STEP SEVEN: To summarize their learning, ask students to complete the following statements, aloud or in writing:

1. List the nine grooming tactics.

2. One question I have is:

Relationship Questionnaire

1. Have you ever touched, pinched, or grabbed someone who did not want you to touch them?

2. Do you make sexual gestures, looks, comments, or jokes in public?

3. Have you ever sent someone unwelcome sexual notes, pictures, or e-mail?

4. Have you ever leaned over or cornered someone who did not welcome your advances?

5. Do you use sexually graphic and vulgar language in front of the opposite gender?

6. Have you ever publicly put down or humiliated someone?

7. Do you reveal private information about others?

8. Do you stand or sit too close to others?

9. Do you ask very personal or sexual questions of people you don't know well?

10. Do you use fights and threats to get your way?

11. Have you ever pressured someone into sexual activity?

12. Have you ever forced someone into sexual activity?

13. Do you believe that sexual behavior is a duty – that a wife owes sex to her husband or vice versa?

14. Have you ever expected someone to pay back a favor owed to you by doing something sexual with you?

15. Do you believe that if you spend a lot of money on a date that your date owes you something sexual in return?

16. Have you given a gift in order to get sex in return?

17. Have you ever treated your boyfriend/girlfriend like an object you own or control? (Telling him or her how to dress, who to hang out with, etc.) ?

18. Have you ever flattered someone in order to get something sexual in return?

19. Have you ever used your status to convince someone to have sex with you?

20. Have you ever used sexual activity to get or keep someone in a relationship with you?

21. Do you take your anger out on others?

22. Do you purposefully attempt to make others feel jealous or insecure?

23. Do you believe that having sex proves something (that you're mature, loyal, cool, etc)?

24. Have you used sexual activity as a way to "make-up" after a fight rather than really working through the original problem?

25. Have you used sexual behavior as a way to feel more powerful over someone else?

26. Have you used sexual behavior as a way to "get back" at someone else?

27. Do you believe that sex and love are the same thing?

Relationship Questionnaire Answer Sheet

I have done			**I have allowed others to do to me**		
1. Yes	No	Sometimes	Yes	No	Sometimes
2. Yes	No	Sometimes	Yes	No	Sometimes
3. Yes	No	Sometimes	Yes	No	Sometimes
4. Yes	No	Sometimes	Yes	No	Sometimes
5. Yes	No	Sometimes	Yes	No	Sometimes
6. Yes	No	Sometimes	Yes	No	Sometimes
7. Yes	No	Sometimes	Yes	No	Sometimes
8. Yes	No	Sometimes	Yes	No	Sometimes
9. Yes	No	Sometimes	Yes	No	Sometimes
10. Yes	No	Sometimes	Yes	No	Sometimes
11. Yes	No	Sometimes	Yes	No	Sometimes
12. Yes	No	Sometimes	Yes	No	Sometimes
13. Yes	No	Sometimes	Yes	No	Sometimes
14. Yes	No	Sometimes	Yes	No	Sometimes
15. Yes	No	Sometimes	Yes	No	Sometimes
16. Yes	No	Sometimes	Yes	No	Sometimes
17. Yes	No	Sometimes	Yes	No	Sometimes
18. Yes	No	Sometimes	Yes	No	Sometimes
19. Yes	No	Sometimes	Yes	No	Sometimes
20. Yes	No	Sometimes	Yes	No	Sometimes
21. Yes	No	Sometimes	Yes	No	Sometimes
22. Yes	No	Sometimes	Yes	No	Sometimes
23. Yes	No	Sometimes	Yes	No	Sometimes
24. Yes	No	Sometimes	Yes	No	Sometimes
25. Yes	No	Sometimes	Yes	No	Sometimes
26. Yes	No	Sometimes	Yes	No	Sometimes
27. Yes	No	Sometimes	Yes	No	Sometimes

Emotional Grooming and the Media

OBJECTIVE: To enable youth to learn how to identify the nine grooming tactics as presented in various forms of contemporary media – TV shows, movies, music, music videos, advertisements – so that youth can better learn how to recognize these tactics in real life situations.

STEP ONE: Begin with a discussion of material that was covered in previous sessions. (Include any pertinent current events that could be used as examples.) You may want to use questions like:

■ What is the most important thing you have learned so far? Why is it important to you?

■ Give an example of an emotional grooming tactic and how it might be used to con someone.

STEP TWO: Distribute the handout "Identifying the Nine Grooming Tactics in Media." Explain that this handout will be used to identify any grooming tactics observed in the media viewed during class.

The following are suggestions for using media presentations with the group:

■ Ask the youth to give examples of what TV programs, videos, or movies they watch or what music they listen to. Then watch these shows and listen to the music

yourself, and identify the tactics that they contain. Decide if you want to use a portion of a TV show, video, or movie, or print out the lyrics of a song to use in class. This same process can be used with magazine articles, advertisements, TV commercials, etc.

■ Avoid using media examples that are extremely offensive or obscene. Sometimes you will have to firmly say "no" to certain shows or songs that a student may suggest. View this as a teaching opportunity; a chance to gently but firmly let youth know what the limits are. Obviously, you will be using contemporary shows and music that contain material related to sex, dating, and relationships. Set firm limits so you are not presenting material that is too sexually explicit or too violent. (Examples of emotional grooming tactics can be found in most prime-time TV sitcoms and dramas, movies that are geared for a teen audience, and Top 40 songs.)

■ Watch a show or listen to a song several times so that you will be prepared to use it with the group.

■ If you use a song or a music video, type out the lyrics and put them on an overhead for use during the discussion.

■ Use segments of TV shows, movies, or songs. Skip parts that do not pertain to emotional grooming tactics. Cue the video or song to what you want to show or play.

Ask the youth to follow these guidelines when watching or listening to media in the classroom. Explain by saying something like:

"It will continue to be very important that we show respect and maturity while viewing media together. We can show respect and maturity by refraining from putdowns, making fun, making negative comments, or laughing during any media presented. It is okay for you to dislike or disagree with what is presented, and it is even okay for you to express your dislike or opposing opinion on something. But you must do this in an appropriate manner by using the skill of Disagreeing Appropriately."

Use this opportunity to teach and practice the steps for "Disagreeing Appropriately." Adapt these steps to fit your group's needs:

1. Look at the person.

2. Use a pleasant tone of voice.

3. Make an empathy/concern

statement like "I understand that you may like this song, but I do not like it because..."

4. Be specific when telling why you disagree.

5. Give a reason for your statement.

6. Say, "Thank you for listening to my opinion."

Continue by explaining:

"When viewing or listening to a media presentation, everyone should listen carefully without talking. You will have time to ask questions or make comments when the video or song is finished. These two behaviors are important so that everyone can give their undivided attention to what is being viewed or listened to and get the most out of the discussions and activities. Once the discussion begins, only one person should speak at a time. Again, this shows respect for the person who is speaking. It also allows everyone an equal chance to hear one another, to voice their own thoughts without being interrupted, and to pay full attention."

Remind youth what kind of language and comments are permitted and what are not.

STEP THREE: Watch (or listen to) media presentations using the handout in this session, "Identifying the Nine Emotional Grooming Tactics in Media." Instruct youth to write down any examples of how the nine grooming tactics were used and by which characters. They may write during or after viewing or listening.

STEP FOUR: After viewing or listening to the media presentation, discuss which grooming tactics the youth observed, how the tactics were used, the effects of these tactics, etc. Practice the skill of "Disagreeing Appropriately" and other important discussion skills before beginning the discussion.

STEP FIVE: Have youth hold a summary discussion or writing activity by answering these questions:

1. Based on the video and music clips presented today and from what you know of contemporary media, are grooming tactics common?

2. Give examples of grooming tactics you've seen in other media.

3. Which tactics do you see used most often? How are they used?

4. Why is it important to be able to recognize these tactics in popular shows and music?

5. How can this information be helpful to you?

One goal of this activity is to have youth begin to recognize the frequency of these messages in the media. Another goal is to realize that these manipulative messages are sometimes portrayed as being characteristic of normal dating and/or marriage.

After the youth have discussed or written their responses to these questions, you also may want them to respond to the following summary statements:

1. Something I learned or realized today is:

2. One question or comment I have is:

3. Something I liked or disliked about today's class was:

4. Other shows, movies, or songs that have emotional grooming themes are:

FOLLOW-UP ACTIVITIES: A good follow-up to analyzing media for examples of emotional grooming activity is to ask students to write a one- to two-page reflection paper describing how exposure to these messages affects the thinking, feeling, and behavior of today's teenagers, especially with regard to relationships with the opposite gender.

Once your class has a clear understanding of each of the nine grooming tactics, have them create role-play situations where they can practice what to say or do if a person tries to use emotional grooming tactics to get them to do something sexual or wrong.

Name_____

Identifying the Nine Grooming Tactics in the Media

DIRECTIONS: Watch each media presentation. Identify and write down examples of characters using any of the following grooming tactics:

Jealousy and possessiveness

Insecurity

Anger

Intimidation

Accusations

Flattery

Status

Bribery

Control

Emotional Grooming Letters

OBJECTIVE: To enable youth to identify how and why emotional grooming tactics are used in teen relationships.

STEP ONE: Begin with the youth's questions and comments from previous sessions. Ask about any examples of grooming they recently observed in the media.

STEP TWO: Explain the session by saying: *"Today, we are going to continue identifying emotional grooming tactics by looking at some notes and letters written by teens to other teens. By carefully analyzing these notes, we can see how the author tries to con the recipient into some sort of unhealthy or abusive relationship. These are real letters written by real young people, both male and female. Their names have been changed to protect their identities."*

TEACHER NOTE: In this lesson there are 30 letters or series of letters provided that illustrate various types of language cons, grooming tactics, and distorted thinking used by emotional groomers. Read through all the letters carefully before choosing which letters you want to use with your group. It is most helpful to create **an overhead transparency** of each letter you will use and then display it on an overhead screen for the group. **Do not** give photocopies of the letters to your class; someone could easily use these letters in an inappropriate manner. Also, note that many of the letters contain sex-ually graphic or offensive language. The language used in each letter, even though often offensive or inappropriate, was left in its original form in order to preserve the authenticity (including grammatical and spelling mistakes). You may choose to black out or delete any language you deem inappropriate. Again, **you** must decide which letters to use. Use only the letters that you decide are appropriate for the age and maturity level of your class. **The grooming letters, in copy-ready format, can be found in the Appendix.**

(Letter #30 refers to youth in an out-of-home setting such as a shelter or group home. It illustrates how carefully a groomer tries to manipulate the target into deceiving their caregivers so their relationship can continue.)

STEP THREE: Distribute and explain how to use the Letters Answer Sheet. Answers for the discussion questions for each of the grooming letters can also be found in the Appendix.

STEP FOUR: Show letters one at a time. Read and discuss each letter using the questions provided. You may ask for student volunteers to read the letters aloud, or you may want to read them aloud yourself. Before reading and discussing letters, remind your students to use the following rules:

1. One person speaks at a time.

2. Show respect for each other's questions and comments by refraining from putdowns.

3. Disagree appropriately.

4. No one will be forced to express thoughts, feelings, or opinions aloud.

STEP FIVE: After reading and discussing several letters, have students summarize by completing the following statements:

1. Something I learned or realized today is:

2. One question or comment I have is:

Name_____

Letters Answer Sheet

**DIRECTIONS: Read the grooming letter shown on the overhead projector.
After reading the letter, discuss the following questions.**

1. Which of the two elements of the grooming process was the author using?
   Describe how.

   a. Developing a false sense of trust

   b. Attempting to keep the relationship secret

2. Which of the nine grooming tactics were used? Give examples from the letter.

   a. Jealousy and possessiveness

   b. Insecurity

   c. Anger

   d. Intimidation

   e. Accusations

   f. Flattery

   g. Status

   h. Bribery

   i. Control

3. How did the author want to make the recipient feel?

   a. Special

   b. Fearful or threatened

   c. Safe

   d. Guilty

   e. Flattered

   f. Obligated

   g. Sorry for him or her

   h. Sexually aroused

   i. Loved

   j. Other_____

4. What did the author want the recipient to do?

    a. To break a rule

    b. To have sex

    c. To feel the same way

    d. To start or continue a relationship

    e. To do what he or she says

    f. To believe everything he or she says

    g. To share his or her feelings

    h. To be the "only one" in this person's life

    i. To keep a secret

    j. Other_____

5. How **should** you respond if you receive a letter like this?

    a. Ignore it and throw it away.

    b. Show it immediately to a trusted adult and ask for help.

    c. Other_____

6. How would your response change if the person sending you this letter were:

    a. A complete stranger. Why?

    b. A casual acquaintance (schoolmate, neighbor). Why?

    c. A friend. Why?

    d. Someone you like or would like to date. Why?

Identifying Distorted Thinking

OBJECTIVE: To enable students to learn what distorted thinking is and to practice identifying various types of thought distortions in grooming letters.

STEP ONE: Begin, as usual, with the youths' questions and comments from previous sessions. Ask about any examples of grooming they recently observed in the media.

STEP TWO: State the objective for this session and explain that this session will be similar to the last session in that you will be analyzing grooming. Ask students to use the same skills used in the last session (See Session 4, Step 4).

STEP THREE: Distribute, read and discuss the handout entitled "Distorted Thinking."

STEP FOUR: Distribute and explain how to use the Distorted Thinking Answer Sheet for this session.

STEP FIVE: Practice identifying thought distortions by reading and analyzing various grooming letters. The teacher should read over letters in the Appendix in advance and choose which letters to use in class. Use only the letters that you decide are appropriate for the age and maturity level of your class. Show one letter at a time and use the questions on the Distorted Thinking Answer Sheet to facilitate discussion.

STEP SIX: After reading, discussing, and analyzing several letters, have the students summarize by completing the following statements:

1. Something I learned or realized today is:

2. One question or comment I have is:

Distorted Thinking

Distorted Thinking is a term used to describe a false, incorrect, or harmful way of thinking. Distorted Thinking is a form of lying to ourselves and others. Distorted Thinking can keep you from seeing things as they really are, from recognizing when someone is trying to hurt or use you, or from admitting that you are hurting or using others.

Emotional groomers and many of their targets engage in Distorted Thinking. Distorted Thinking is dangerous! It's a lie and a con and always a sign of an unhealthy relationship.

There are many types of distorted thinking. We are going to focus on some of the types most commonly used by groomers.

■ Filtering

■ Overgeneralization

■ Control Fallacies

■ Emotional Reasoning

FILTERING
To have tunnel vision, to magnify or "awfulize" your thoughts.

Examples of filtering:

"The reason why I deaded this relationships is because there was too much s--- going on. People were telling me that you and Kyle had something going on. And a lot of guys flirt with you and you don't care."

"You're so very special. I wish I was special, but I'm a creep. I'm a whiner. What the hell am I doing here? I don't belong here!"

"My life is hell. I'm just gonna give up on guys cuz I like Dwayne and I can tell he doesn't like me, so, f--- all of them damn pigs."

OVERGENERALIZATION
To make a broad generalized conclusion based on a single incident or piece of information. Key words include: always, never, none, all, everybody.

Examples of overgeneralization:

*"Why would I cheat on you? But that's fine – you want to leave me. I guess the rumors are right. Boys are **nothing** but players."*

*"Well, I'm kinda bummed cuz I don't want them breaking us apart. The **only** thing keeping me here is you. The **only** thing keeping me from having an emotional breakdown is you."*

*"I just wanted to tell you that I love you very much! I don't care what other people say or do, I'm **never** gonna stop loving you. You complete me. I'm not me without you. No matter how many other guys or girls there are, they can **never** change my feelings for you."*

CONTROL FALLACIES
To see yourself as helpless and externally controlled or omnipotent and responsible for everyone around you.

Examples of control fallacies:

*"About my hair, I'm sorry. My hair just grows fast. And I don't like it on my shoulders or on my back. But, if **you** don't like my hair short I will grow it all out."*

*"If you really want me you would **do everything I ask you to**."*

*"I am so disappointed. I can't believe you got in trouble last night. You've gotta promise, pinky swear, that while I'm gone you'll be good and try your best not to go off, to not get mad, to control your anger. Please don't make me worry about you. Just be a good boy – **for me**."*

EMOTIONAL REASONING
To believe that whatever you're feeling must be true.

Examples of emotional reasoning:

"Do you want to know something? The way I feel for you is stronger than anything I've ever felt. I love you more than I ever loved or could love anyone else."

"I also know you don't have the heart to hit anyone. You have proven to me that you are too much of a sweetheart for that kind of abuse."

"When I look in your eyes I knew it was true. My heart never lies, I was in love with you."

Distorted Thinking Answer Sheet

DIRECTIONS: Read the grooming letter displayed on the overhead transparency. Then answer the following questions.

1. Which types of **distorted thinking** can you identify in this letter? Cite examples.

   a. Filtering

   b. Overgeneralization

   c. Control Fallacies

   d. Emotional Reasoning

2. Write below an example of distorted thinking found in this letter.

3. Which type of distorted thinking is this?

4. What is distorted or false about this statement?

5. What could go wrong if you believed this kind of distorted thinking?

6. Write an honest response to this thought distortion, pointing out how it is false, distorted, or harmful to you.

session

Boundaries for Healthy Relationships

OBJECTIVE: To enable students to better understand what personal boundaries are and how to establish healthy boundaries in all relationships. (This session may take more that one class period to complete.)

STEP ONE: Begin by asking for any questions or comments about the previous session.

STEP TWO: Ask the group, *"What's the purpose of a fence?"* (Keeps things in, keeps things out, tells you where your property begins and ends, safety, protection, privacy, etc).

Summarize by repeating any of their answers and adding those listed above.

Continue by explaining:

"A fence is an example of a boundary. I used the example of a fence to get you to think about your personal boundaries – why you have them and what purpose they serve in order to help you. During the rest of this session we are going to focus on obtaining a better understanding of what personal boundaries are and learning how to establish healthy boundaries in all your relationships.

"Everyone has some sort of boundaries. Even though we can't really see them, our boundaries are there to protect us and keep us safe from emotional or physical harm. We first learn boundaries from our parents and other significant adults in our lives. We often learn what a boundary should be without even knowing that we are learning it. Sometimes,

though, our parents actually do tell us what our boundaries should be. Can you tell me about a time when your Mom or Dad told you what to do or not to do with strangers?" (Allow the youth to respond.) Then ask, *"Why do you think your parents told you that?"* (Allow time for their answers.)

"Your parents told you what to do or not do with strangers because they were trying to protect you. They were teaching you about the kinds of boundaries you should have with strangers. Can you think of any other things your Mom, Dad, or another important adult has told you about what to do or not do with other people?" (As they name different things they were told, identify and affirm any statements that are examples of appropriate boundaries.)

STEP THREE: Explain that they are now going to read and discuss more about boundaries. Ask students to open to the Boundaries chapter of their Teen's Guide. Spend as much time as students need to read pages 45-56 and discuss thoroughly. Remember to stop after every paragraph or two and ask for questions or comments from the group. You may also want to point out the sections or sentences you'd like them to highlight for future reference.

STEP FOUR: After reading and discussing the chapter on Boundaries, make the following summarizing points the students can take down as notes:

■ There are two types of boundaries, external and internal.

■ External boundaries are broken into two categories – physical and sexual. (Give examples.)

■ Internal boundaries have two categories also, emotional and spiritual. (Give examples.)

■ Boundaries work in two ways:

1. They allow things and people in. (Give examples.)

2. They also keep things and people out. (Give examples.)

   ■ Some people's boundaries are too closed and some are too open. (Give examples.)

   ■ Appropriate boundaries help us have good and healthy friendships and relationships.

   ■ Paying attention to our boundaries can help us not get hurt or used by others and to not hurt or use others.

STEP FIVE: Show the overhead of the Boundary Circles. Explain by saying,

"These concentric circles represent all the different kinds of relationships and boundaries we have in life: from strangers at the outermost circle to the most intimate of relationships (spouse) in the inner circle. Place yourself in the center of all the circles. The circles closest to

the center (you) represent the most private and special emotional, spiritual, physical, and sexual parts of who you are, parts of you which should be shared only with a limited number of trustworthy, loving, and caring people. Notice that each of the outer circles is farther and farther away from the most private parts of you. This is important. Only certain people should get close to you, both physically and emotionally. Your emotional and physical boundaries protect you and help you keep a manipulative person from getting too close.

"If the wrong sort of person does get too close, your boundaries can warn you of possible harm or danger. How do your boundaries warn you? Usually, you will feel uncomfortable, scared, nervous, very uncertain, or anxious about a person or an experience that is not good for you. You should trust these inner feelings. They are trying to warn you and protect you from possible hurt or abuse. When you notice those feelings, talk to a trusted adult. Tell the adult what is going on, and ask for help and insights. Then you will begin to see the danger more clearly, and be able to decide what you should do about it.

"Sometimes, you may not pay enough attention to your feelings; in those situations, a friend or family member may sound the first warning. Again, you should listen to the people who care about you and who have earned your trust and respect. They may see something that you don't see. They may notice a potentially dangerous situation before you do. Again, open up to their comments, talk about what is really happening, and look at things from their perspective. Remember, they are only trying to protect you and show care and concern for your well-being."

STEP SIX: Distribute and explain the Boundary Circles Worksheet and Reflection Questions. Give time to complete.

Boundary Circles

SELF

Most intimate – *spouse*

Intimate – *very close family member or friend*

Close – *friend or family member*

Superficial – *acquaintance, classmate, neighbor*

Extremely superficial – *stranger*

Your Boundary Circles Worksheet

To understand boundaries better, imagine a series of concentric circles surrounding you. These circles represent various kinds of boundaries and relationships and can help you picture how close you will let someone get to you – emotionally, spiritually, sexually, and physically.

Everyone you encounter fits somewhere in these boundary circles. Strangers are the farthest outside while your family and a few very close friends may be closest to you.

Where do the various people in your life fit within your Boundary Circles? Write their names in the appropriate places.

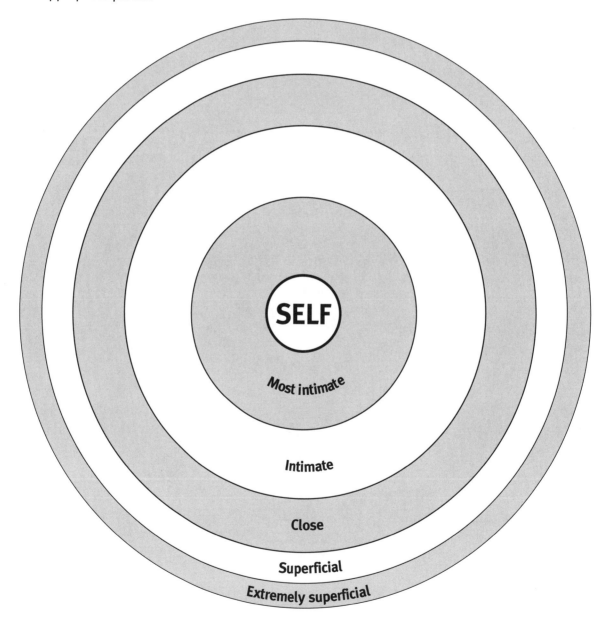

Boundary Circles Reflection Questions

DIRECTIONS: Use your personal "Boundary Circles" and the information given during class to help you answer these questions.

1. Whose names are listed closest to the center of your boundary circles? Explain why these people are allowed to be closest to you.

2. Who or what kinds of relationships are listed farthest from the center of your boundary circles? Explain why.

3. What are the two components of external boundaries? Give an example of each.

4. What are the two components of internal boundaries?
   Give an example of each.

5. Explain how appropriate boundaries can help you have appropriate relationships.

Rules for Good Boundaries

Objective: To enable students to understand how having healthy boundaries can help them have more appropriate friendships and dating relationships.

STEP ONE: Discuss the students' responses to the Boundary Circles Reflection Questions from the previous session.

STEP TWO: Explain, *"In the previous session we learned about what boundaries are and how they can help you have healthier relationships. Today's session will help you discover more about how healthy boundaries can help you have more appropriate friendships and dating relationships."*

STEP THREE: Ask the class, *"When does a stranger become an acquaintance? When does an acquaintance become a friend?"*

Allow students to struggle with and discuss these two questions. Explain that knowing your boundaries and respecting others' boundaries help us to know when and how to go forward in relationships.

Distribute the handout, "Rules for Good Boundaries" (also found on pages 56-62 of the Teen's Guide). Explain that these rules are questions we can ask ourselves that will help us have healthier friendships and dating relationships. Read and discuss the handout together.

STEP FOUR: After discussion, distribute and explain the Boundaries Reflection Questions Worksheet. Allow time to complete. Then discuss their responses.

STEP FIVE: Distribute and explain the Homework Worksheet, "How Do People Violate Boundaries?" Give time to complete and discuss or assign the worksheet as homework.

Rules for Good Boundaries

1. **Length of time** – How long have you known this person? How can knowing someone longer be beneficial to you? How long is long enough before a stranger becomes a friend? How do you decide?

2. **Knowledge about the other person** – What, and how much, do you really know about this person? Some important things to know about someone you are considering dating are:

    ■ How this person reacts when given "no" for an answer.

    ■ How this person handles frustrations and disappointments.

    ■ How he or she expresses anger.

    ■ How this person treats his or her parents.

    ■ How this person speaks about and treats the other gender.

    How can this knowledge help you make good choices in a relationship? Explain or give examples.

3. **Sharing activities** – How many different kinds of activities have you shared together? What are they? How have these experiences helped you get to know the other person better?

4. **Amount of self-disclosure** – How much personal information have you shared? How much has the other person shared? Are you comfortable with the sharing? Why or why not? Is the amount of sharing equal between the two of you?

5. **Number of different experiences** – What has this person experienced in life? How has it affected him or her? What can these experiences tell you about him or her?

6. **Role appropriate** – We all have certain roles in life. Some roles are incompatible for dating or friendship relationships. Teachers don't date students, doctors don't date patients, etc. What role does this person have in your life?

7. **Age appropriate** – As adolescents, friendships or dating relationships with those two or more years older or younger than us can be harmful. What is the age difference between you? If more than two years, how could this be harmful?

8. **Level of reciprocal trust** – Can I trust this person? How do I know? Am I worthy of his or her trust? Why? How do you know when someone is trustworthy? What happens when trust is broken?

9. **Level of commitment** – Some types of commitments are harmful or detrimental to teens. What kind of commitments are appropriate for your age? Ask your parents and other trusted adults for guidance and counsel in this area.

Name_____

Boundaries Reflection Questions

DIRECTIONS: Based on the boundary information presented in the last two sessions, answer the following questions.

1. Which of the Rules for Good Boundaries do you need to put into practice to help you have healthier

    a. friendships? Why?

    b. dating relationships? Why?

    c. family relationships? Why?

2. Which rule do you most need to put into practice in your life right now?

3. How will this rule help you?

4. Who or what could help you put this rule into practice?

Name_____

How Do People Violate Boundaries?

Read this list of boundary violations:

Interrupting a conversation.

Taking someone's possessions without his or her permission.

Teasing or making fun of someone.

Asking very personal questions.

Telling other people stories about someone.

Telling other people private information about yourself.

Making someone uncomfortable by always being around or invading his or her private space.

Saying or doing things that others find offensive or vulgar.

Forcing someone into doing something sexual.

Physically abusing someone.

Using inappropriate language or touching.

Abusing someone in any way.

Follow these instructions:

First, place a check mark next to any statement listed above that has happened to you. Then, underline the statements above that describe what you have done to someone else.

Answer these questions:

1. How does violating another's boundaries hurt that person? Explain.

2. How does violating someone else's boundaries affect you? Explain.

3. What can you do to make amends for the times you have violated the boundaries of others?

4. If someone is constantly violating your boundaries, what should you do?

How Do People Violate Boundaries?

1. How does violating another's boundaries hurt that person? Explain.

   Breaking someone's boundary shows disrespect and can harm him or her emotionally and physically.

2. How does violating someone else's boundaries affect you? Explain.

   May make me less sensitive and caring toward others. Makes it difficult for me to learn good boundaries for myself. Is hurtful to others, so could make me feel guilty and ashamed.

3. What can you do to make amends for the times you have violated the boundaries of others?

   Ask for forgiveness from them. Learn more about boundaries and respect them.

4. If someone is constantly violating your boundaries, what should you do?

   Talk to a trusted adult for advice. Recognize that it is not a healthy relationship and that I should get out of it.

The 12 Steps of Physical Closeness

OBJECTIVE: To enable students to understand and apply the 12 Steps of Physical Closeness to healthy relationships.

NOTE: This session may take more than one class period to complete.

PREPARATION:

- List each of the 12 Steps of Physical Closeness separately in large bold print on sheets of 8 1/2 in. x 11 in. paper. Do not number each step. Then laminate each sheet, thus creating a mini-poster of each of the 12 steps.

- Use Proactive Teaching to prepare students for the special content of this session. (See Chapter 9.)

- Create an overhead of the 12 steps (provided with this lesson plan).

STEP ONE: State objective for today's class by saying:

"Today's session will introduce you to the 12 Steps of Physical Closeness. These steps are one way of understanding some of what happens between two people as they get physically closer to one another. Remember that physical closeness is not the same as emotional or spiritual closeness, though physical closeness can produce strong emotional responses in people. Understanding and respecting these

12 steps can help you to have more healthy and respectful relationships."

STEP TWO: Ask for 12 volunteers. Give each volunteer a laminated sheet containing one of the 12 Steps of Physical Closeness. Explain to the class and the volunteers that each student has one of the 12 Steps of Physical Closeness, and that their task is to come to the front of the room and line up in order as to which step they believe should be the first, second, third, and so on, in a developing male-female relationship. The rest of the class can help by giving the volunteers suggestions. Allow for some frustration and confusion, as this may be new and/or embarrassing information for some youth.

Call "time" after about five minutes. At this point have volunteers remain where they are lined up. Then rearrange volunteers as needed to help them get into the correct order.

Volunteers can continue standing and holding their steps in order – or you may have volunteers tape their steps to the wall in the correct order.

STEP THREE: Explain the 12 Steps of Physical Closeness as follows:

Step 1: Eye to Body – The first thing we notice about another person is the body; the physical being. It is the first form of acknowledging another person. This step can be sexual or nonsexual, depending on the context. Noticing someone is a nonsexual example of eye to body, looking someone over or "checking them out" is a more sexual example of this step.

Step 2: Eye to Eye – The next step in getting to know someone is to look them in the eye or to make eye contact. This step can be sexual or nonsexual, depending on the context. Nonsexual eye to eye contact happens all the time, whenever you look someone in the eye. A more sexual example of eye to eye is winking or staring.

Step 3: Voice to Voice – This step involves talking to the other person – introducing yourself. Having a conversation with that person helps you get to know more about the other person. This is a crucial step. Much time should be spent on this step. This is the step that helps us decide whether or not we want to, or should, get physically or emotionally closer to the other person. A good guideline is that one should spend 300 hours at this step before going any further. These 300 hours of conversation need to happen in person or over the phone, but not via e-mail, instant messaging, or in chat rooms. Given that 70 per cent of communication happens nonverbally, much of the real content of the conversation is missed when communicating via the Internet. Also note that these 300 hours of conversation need to be nonsexual in nature. Once the conversation includes sexual content, you have skipped ahead many steps and the relationship will suffer.

Step 4: Hand to Hand – Again, this step can be sexual or nonsexual, depending on the context. An example of a more sexually intimate contact – holding hands on a date. A nonsexual example would be shaking hands when you meet someone.

Step 5: Arm to Shoulder – Once again, this step can be sexual or nonsexual in nature. A more sexually intimate example – a young man puts his arm around the shoulder of his date. A nonsexual example – a coach gives an athlete a pat on the back.

Step 6: Arm to Waist – This step is more physically intimate but still not always sexual in nature. Two examples of step 6 are hugging and slow dancing. Though hugging is not always sexually intimate, it is more physically intimate. We should only hug people that we feel close to and comfortable with. Hugging can obviously be sexual or nonsexual.

Step 7: Face to Face – This step usually involves kissing. It is definitely more physically intimate, although not always sexual in nature. A nonsexual example of step 7 is a parent kissing a child.

Step 8: Hand to Face – This usually goes along with step 7. When we kiss someone, whether it is a sexual or nonsexual kiss, we often touch his or her face, head, or hair. Touching the face or head is a very intimate gesture. Think about it. Who do you allow to touch your face? Usually only those people you feel very close to and comfortable with. Though touching someone's face is a very physically intimate gesture, there are a few nonsexual examples – a mother touching the forehead of a sick child or a dentist working on a patient's teeth.

Step 9: Hand to Body, Over Clothes – Obviously, there is a significant shift in the level of physical closeness between steps 8 and 9. Once we engage in step 9, each following step will become more physically and sexually involved. There may be a few nonsexual examples of step 9, but not many (being frisked by a police officer). Step 9 almost always involves sexual intimacy.

Step 10: Touching above Waist, Under Clothes – This is a much more physically and sexually intimate step. It most likely will only occur in a sexual context. The only exception might be a doctor examining a patient.

Step 11: Touching below Waist, Under Clothes – Again, this is an extremely physically and sexually intimate behavior that has definite physical, sexual, and emotional responses and consequences. Although male and female responses may be very differ-

ent, both will have strong responses to this step.

Step 12: Intercourse-Vaginal, Oral and Anal – It may seem unnecessary to be so specific. However, current studies show that many adolescents, especially 12- to 15-year-olds, do not consider oral and anal sex to be sex. We must help teens understand that although pregnancy may be avoided by practicing these two behaviors, other emotional, physical, and spiritual consequences will be similar to vaginal intercourse.

Show the overhead (found in this lesson plan) of the 12 Steps of Physical Closeness and have students take notes based on the following points:

- Copy each of the steps as listed on the overhead.

- Notice that on the overhead steps 9-12 are boxed off and not named specifically. This box reminds us of three things:

  1. The 12 Steps of Physical Closeness are progressive in nature. With each step we are becoming more physically and usually more sexually involved. This physical closeness may produce an emotional closeness in some people, especially females. This can be dangerous because it could be a false sense of emotional closeness – sometimes called bonding – that is not shared by both persons or not based on the right things. Steps 1-8 can bring two people physically closer in sexual or nonsexual ways, but once a couple

engages in steps 9-12, they have crossed a line where their behaviors now are extremely physical and sexual in nature.

2. When people engage in steps 9-12, there are definite, predictable, and sometimes unavoidable physical responses and consequences. Once a couple engages in steps 9-12 it becomes increasingly more difficult to stop and people are more physically driven to want to go all the way to step 12. Note that it is **always** possible to stop at any step – but it becomes much more difficult the further along a couple progresses.

3. To protect virginity and achieve chastity, steps 9-12 should be reserved for married couples only. The box around steps 9-12 reminds us that these steps of physical closeness are best reserved for marriage.

Make one last point about the steps of physical closeness: The steps are just one way of thinking about how physical behaviors can produce a sense of emotional and spiritual closeness – or bonding – between two people.

STEP FOUR: Distribute and explain the Reflection Questions Worksheet. Give time to complete. Then discuss student responses.

STEP FIVE: Distribute and explain the Homework Worksheet.

OPTIONAL HOMEWORK ASSIGNMENT: Instruct the students to explain the 12 Steps of Physical Closeness to their parents and to ask their parents:

- How far (to what step) would you want me to go in a male-female friendship? Why?

- How far would you want me to go in a casual dating relationship? Why?

- How far would you want me to go in a serious dating relationship? Why?

- Which steps should be reserved for marriage? Why?

Sources: Information on the 12 Steps of Physical Closeness has been adapted from the Steps to Intimacy in *Intimate Behavior* by Desmond Morris, Random House, 1971, the Second Edition of *Bonding: Relationships in the Image of God,* by Donald M. Joy, Ph.D., 1999, Evangel Publishing House, pp. 32-55, and the WAIT Training curriculum, available from the National Abstinence Training Center, 2938 Cottesford Way, Smyrna, GA, 30080.

The 12 Steps of Physical Closeness

Reflection Questions

1. How far (which step) is far enough for a first date? Why? How would your parents answer this question? Why?

2. How far is **too far** for a first date? Why? How would your parents answer this question? Why?

3. How far is **far enough** before marriage? Why? How would your parents answer this question? Why?

4. How will you communicate these decisions to the guys/girls you date?

5. How will you prevent yourself from being tempted to go too far?

6. What can you do to avoid giving others the message that you're willing to put out?

7. Should you talk about the 12 steps and your limits with a guy/girl you are interested in dating? How will you bring it up? What will you say?

8. What kinds of things **should** you be talking about during the 300 hours of conversation before hand holding?

9. How will you decide if you should date a certain guy/girl or not?

10. What are some of the possible negative consequences of sexually bonding (going too far) with someone you are **not** married to?

12 Steps of Physical Closeness Homework

DIRECTIONS: You may use your notes to help you answer the following questions.

1. Name and explain the three reasons why steps 9-12 are boxed off into their own
    category.

    a.

    b.

    c.

2. How can knowing about the 12 Steps of Physical Closeness help you have more
    appropriate relationships?

12 Steps of Physical Closeness Homework

1. Name and explain the three reasons why steps 9-12 are boxed off into their own category.

   a. *Steps 9-12 cross a line. They are much more sexually intimate than 1-8.*

   b. *Steps 9-12 should be reserved for marriage only, thus protecting virginity and achieving chastity.*

   c. *When couples engage in any of steps 9-12, it becomes much more difficult to stop, especially more difficult than steps 1-8.*

2. How can knowing about the 12 Steps of Physical Closeness help you have more appropriate relationships?

   Can help me set better limits for friendships and dating relationships.

   Can help me show respect for myself and for my date.

The 12 Steps of Physical Closeness

1. Eye to Body

2. Eye to Eye

3. Voice to Voice

4. Hand to Hand

5. Hand to Shoulder

6. Hand to Waist

7. Face to Face

8. Hand to Face

9-12. Reserved for Marriage

Grooming, Boundaries, and the 12 Steps

OBJECTIVE: To analyze the grooming letters in order to practice recognizing various grooming tactics and boundary violations and how they correlate to the 12 Steps of Physical Closeness.

STEP ONE: Review by having students name and list on the board:

- The nine Grooming Tactics (anger, insecurity, jealousy and possessiveness, intimidation, accusations, control, bribery, status, flattery)

- The four types of Boundaries (physical, sexual, emotional, spiritual)

- The 12 Steps of Physical Closeness (see previous session)

STEP TWO: State the objective for today's session. Explain by saying, *"Today we are going to look at more of the grooming letters, but this time when we analyze the letters we are going to combine all that we have learned so far. This time we will be looking for:*

- *Which of the nine Grooming Tactics were used.*

- *Which of the four types of Boundaries were crossed.*

- *Where on the 12 Steps of Physical Closeness does the groomer want the target to go and how that would harm the target."*

STEP FOUR: Distribute and explain the worksheet for this session. Show selected grooming letters one at a time on the overhead projector. Use the worksheet to analyze each letter.

STEP FIVE: After analyzing letters, ask students to write a one-page paper describing what they have learned so far and how the information will help them in future relationships.

STEP SIX: For homework, direct students to read Chapter 6 of the Teen's Guide, "Friendship and Dating Skills."

Name_____

Grooming, Boundaries, and the 12 Steps

DIRECTIONS: For each of the letters read, answer the following questions.

1. Which of the nine Grooming Tactics did you observe in this letter? Explain.

2. Which of the four types of Boundaries were crossed by what the author wrote? Explain.

3. To which step of the 12 Steps of Physical Closeness did the author want the recipient to go? How would this be harmful to the target?

Friendship and Dating Skills

OBJECTIVE: To enable students to identify skills that will help them have healthy friendships and dating relationships.

PREPARATION: For this session you may find it helpful to have to a copy of *Teaching Social Skills to Youth,* by Tom Dowd and Jeff Tierney, 1992 (available from the Boys Town Press, 1-800-282-6657).

STEP ONE: The Golden Rule Activity

Create a large T-chart on poster paper or chalkboard. Title one column "How I want to be treated by the other gender" and title the other column "How I do **not** want to be treated by the other gender."

Divide class into same gender small groups. Direct each small group to complete their own T-chart. Instruct them to be as specific as possible when listing examples. For example, don't just write the word *disrespect* – describe the specific words and behaviors that show disrespect to your gender – e.g., sexual name calling, grabbing, pinching, cat calls, whistles, etc. Encourage youth to see this as a chance to teach the other gender how to treat them.

Give ample time to complete T-charts. Make sure to circulate among the groups, challenging them to be as specific as possible. Post T-charts around room. Invite a representative from each small group to explain their T-chart.

Once all explanations are complete, ask the class to compare and contrast the contents of the T-charts. Ask:

■   What similarities do you notice between the males' and females' lists?

■   Does anything on the other gender's list surprise you? Why?

■   Why do you think this is called the Golden Rule activity? (The Golden Rule states that we should treat others the way we want to be treated. That's exactly what this activity helps us to see – that males and females generally do want similar treatment.)

STEP TWO: Make the following points about the Golden Rule activity:

■   Note the general similarities between the two lists. Most males and females really want the same thing – to be treated with respect. We may describe respect a little differently, but it is respect we desire.

- Setting your own boundaries and recognizing others' boundaries will help you show respect to others and show others that you also deserve respect.

STEP THREE: Distribute the List of Skills Handout. Ask students to circle the skills they need in order to have good friendships and dating relationships. Give ample time for students to look over skills list. As a large group, discuss their response to the handout by asking:

- Which skills are needed in friendships? Why?

- Which skills are needed in dating relationships? Why?

- Are any skills missing? What would you call that skill? Why would it be an important skill for friendship or dating?

STEP FOUR: Summarize by making the following points:

- Each of these skills is important for both friendships and dating because friendship is the foundation for any healthy dating relationship. (More on this in Step 5.)

- Each skill listed has various skill components – or steps. Show a few examples on overhead transparencies or on posters. (Examples can be found at the end of Chapter 9 or in the *Teaching Social Skills to Youth* book mentioned at the beginning of this session.)

- Once students have seen a few examples of the steps of various

skills, ask them if there are any skills listed on the handout that they do not know how to do – in other words, which skills do they need to know the specific components of. Make a list of these skills. Tell students that you will take this list and create handouts of the skills steps that they need. (Once again, you can copy these directly from the *Teaching Social Skills to Youth* book.)

STEP FIVE: Make the connection between friendship and dating by showing the Dating Steps overhead and make the following points:

- Dating is first and foremost a type of friendship. It is not supposed to be a sexually intimate relationship.

- The purpose of dating is to learn how to be friends with and have fun with members of the other gender. Ultimately, for most people, the purpose of dating is to find a suitable spouse.

- Friendship is also the foundation for any good marriage. If your spouse is not first and foremost your friend, chances are slim that your marriage will last. Contrary to popular beliefs, it is good friendship skills, not sexual skills, that will help your marriage stand the test of time.

- The foundation for any healthy dating relationship is learning how to be a friend and have friends. That's why **the first two steps involve friendship.** First you have to learn how to be friends with those of your gender. Second, you must learn to be purely platonic friends (nothing sexual involved) with those of the other gender. It is only when you have mastered the skills needed for these two steps, that you can proceed to step 3.

- In order to participate in Step 3 – Friendly Dating, you must establish your specific physical, emotional, sexual, and spiritual boundaries, and you must be able to communicate these boundaries to those you will date. The 12 Steps of Physical Closeness can be very helpful here.

- Step 4 – Steady Friendly Dating describes the type of steady dating that, if it happens, usually happens in high school. Most high school teens are not and should not be thinking about marriage yet. They know that they have more to learn, experience, and achieve in life before they'll be ready to settle down. They know they are not yet ready for step 5 – not yet ready to be asking the question, "Is this the spouse for me?" Yet, rather than dating several different people, some teens may be ready to develop a deeper, emotionally closer dating relationship with one person. This is steady friendly dating. It is important to stress to teens involved in this type of dating that the temptation to go "too far" sexually will most likely increase in this type of relationship. Because the amount of time spent together increases and because the two are most likely

connecting on a deeper emotional level, the desire to be physically closer will also grow. Teens who are ready for this type of dating relationship demonstrate the following skills: They are able to set and communicate clear boundaries and limits, exhibit self-control, resist peer pressure, handle sexuality appropriately, handle frustrations appropriately, express feelings appropriately, show self-respect and respect for others.

- Step 5 – Serious Steady Dating usually occurs in late teens, young adulthood, and beyond. This is when a person begins to ask: "Is this the spouse for me? Do I really love this person? Does he or she really love me?" It is at this step that the couple begins to examine the relationship in light of marriage. All the skills listed above are necessary for this level of dating. Just as in steady friendly dating, it is extremely important to maintain clear and appropriate sexual, emotional, physical, and spiritual boundaries so that each person can make good decisions about the future of the relationship.

- Step 6 – Engagement. During this time the couple should begin preparations for sharing a life together. Discussions about finances, in-laws, conflict resolution, child rearing, etc., need to happen now. The focus should be on preparing for the future, not just for the wedding day. Again, it is very important for the couple to set and maintain clear and firm boundaries. The temptation to go further sexually will again crop up. Remember, engagement is not the same as marriage. Many engagements do not result in marriage. Now is not the time to relax your boundaries.

■ For most people, Step 7 – Marriage is the ultimate goal of dating. If all the previous steps have been taken, friendship skills have been mastered, and appropriate boundaries have been maintained, the couple will have an excellent chance of achieving a lasting, loving marriage.

STEP SIX: Ask students to write a one-page reflection paper summarizing what they have learned in this session.

Name_____

List of Skills

DIRECTIONS: Read through the skills listed below. Circle any skill you would need to know how to do in order to have healthy friendships and dating relationships.

1. Greet someone/introduce yourself
2. Ask for a date
3. Make a request
4. Accept "no" for an answer
5. Accept criticism
6. Accept consequences
7. Disagree appropriately
8. Resist peer pressure
9. Say "no" effectively
10. Apologize
11. Accept an apology
12. Give a compliment
13. Accept a compliment
14. Engage in a conversation
15. Solve problems
16. Show respect
17. Respect someone else's boundaries
18. Use self-control
19. Express feelings appropriately
20. Ask for help
21. Handle anger appropriately
22. Control your emotions
23. Handle sexuality appropriately
24. Recognize and respond to those in need
25. Interact appropriately with members of the other gender
26. Express affection appropriately

Dating Steps

MARRIAGE
Bonding on all levels –
emotional, physical, sexual
and spiritual.

7

ENGAGEMENT
Couple prepares for life-long,
committed, bonded relationship.

6

SERIOUS STEADY DATING
Is this the spouse for me? Begin examining
relationship in light of marriage. Maintains
same boundaries listed below.

5

STEADY FRIENDLY DATING
Dating one person exclusively while maintaining
appropriate emotional and sexual boundaries.
Goes no further than Steps 6-8 of Physical Closeness.

4

FRIENDLY DATING
Includes group dating and single dating. Purpose is to get to know
many different people. Helps to shape your idea of who you might
want to date seriously. It is wise to go no further than Step 6 of
Physical Closeness.

3

OPPOSITE-GENDER FRIENDS
Learn and practice how to have fun with and appreciate the other gender.

2

SAME-GENDER FRIENDS
Learn and practice what it means to be a genuine friend.

1

Mask-Making Activity

OBJECTIVE: To enable students who have completed the *Unmasking Sexual Con Games* curriculum to summarize what they have learned about healthy and unhealthy relationships.

STEP ONE: Choose a method of mask making.

Below are two options for materials used to make the masks. You can offer one or both options to your students, as you see fit.

Plaster of Paris Masks

Materials needed:

- Plaster of Paris cloth, cut into 5 in. x 2 in. strips

- Scissors

- Plastic containers for water and paintbrushes

- Paints and brushes

- Vaseline

- Towels and rags

- Aprons or old T-shirts (to protect clothing)

- Old pillows

- Facial cleansing soap

- Cotton balls

Painting on Plastic Mask Forms

Materials needed:

- Plastic mask forms (available at arts and crafts stores)

- Acrylic paints

- Old T-shirts or aprons (for youth to wear when painting)

- Old newspapers or drop cloths (to protect desks and floors)

- Paintbrushes

- Containers for water

- Paper towels or cloth rags (for cleanup)

STEP TWO: Explain the objective of this activity and how the activity will proceed. Say something like:

"Mask making is a summary activity designed to help you express what you have learned or realized as a result of reading and discussing the Unmasking Sexual Con Games curriculum. Each mask is to be the face of a target or of a groomer. The expression on the face of the mask, the colors used, and any

symbols dawn or painted on the mask should somehow express what it feels like to be a target of grooming OR how the groomer wants to appear in order to best con someone else."

It may be helpful to show examples of masks made by others who have completed this program or show the examples found in the Teacher's Manual. After creating masks, students will be asked to complete reflection questions that will enable them to put into words what they are expressing symbolically in their mask.

STEP THREE: Inform students of the materials they need to provide and the amount of time allocated to complete the activity. (Painting on plastic masks could be completed in one extended session. Plaster of Paris mask making will take longer to complete, probably two sessions – one to create masks and one to paint masks, with 24-hour drying time between creating and painting. Each student will need to bring an old T-shirt or apron to wear while creating or painting masks. (Students serving as plaster of Paris mask models should bring their own facial soap and towel for personal cleanup.)

STEP FOUR: Create plaster of Paris masks according to the following instructions. Go directly to Step Five if plastic masks are being used.

In order to make a plaster of Paris mask, there must be a mask model. A mask model is someone who is willing to have plaster of Paris applied to his or her face as a mold for the mask. Here's how the process works:

1. Mask model puts on old T-shirt over clothes, pulls or pins back hair,

washes face and removes any facial oils or make-up.

2. Next apply a coat of Vaseline all over the model's face. Make sure to apply to the edge of the hairline and under the chin. The Vaseline prevents the plaster of Paris from sticking to the face or hair.

3. The model then sits in a chair and tilts his or her head back, or lies on the floor with a pillow under the head and cotton balls in the ears to absorb any drippings.

4. The model's partner now applies 5 in. x 2 in. strips of plaster of Paris to the model's face.

   ■ Just before applying, dip each strip into a container of water and moisten thoroughly.

   ■ Apply strips to model's face.

   ■ Cover the face completely, even the eyes. (Eyes must be closed!) Make sure to cover the face to every edge and even under the chin. Cover the bridge of the nose but not the nostrils. Nostrils on the mask can be covered later after mask is off the model and dried.

   ■ Apply about three layers of strips. Smooth as you apply.

   ■ Let mask set on model's face for about 7 – 10 minutes.

   ■ When mask feels hardened, have model lean forward while gently loosening mask from face. Mask should come off fairly easily. Set mask on table to continue drying.

- Mask model should then wash his or her face.

- Allow masks to dry overnight, then follow instructions for painting masks.

STEP FIVE: Paint masks following the instructions below.

- Make sure each youth has a mask and needed materials. Remind students to depict either the face of a target – what it feels like to be groomed, or to depict the face of a groomer – what a groomer hides behind in order to con someone into being used.

- Provide paints, brushes, water containers for cleaning brushes, rags for spills, etc. Make sure students paint over drop cloths and wear old T-shirts or aprons while painting to protect their clothing.

- Make sure students paint their names or initials inside their masks so they are not mixed up later on.

STEP SIX: After the masks are painted, have each student seriously and thoughtfully complete the Mask Reflection Questions Worksheet. When all masks and worksheets are completed, invite students to show and tell one another about their masks.

Name_____

Mask Reflection Questions

DIRECTIONS: Please seriously and thoughtfully answer the following questions based on the mask you created.

1. Describe your mask and what it symbolizes.

2. If my mask could talk it would say:

3. My mask is hiding:

4. Explain how you hurt yourself or others when you choose to wear any kind of "mask."

5. Instead of wearing the mask of a groomer or a target, in my future relationships I am going to:

APPENDIX

Emotional Grooming Letters

The following letters illustrate various types of language cons, grooming tactics, and distorted thinking used by emotional groomers. These are **real** letters, confiscated from groomers or their targets. In order to retain authenticity. the letters are presented with the original grammatical and spelling mistakes as well as some **graphic sexual language.** This offensive and vulgar language is not included for shock value, but to show the reality of the language heard and spoken among some teens today.

The grooming letters are included and intended for use as a teaching and learning activity. Using real letters enables students to more readily identify the language, tactics, and distorted thinking employed by groomers to con and manipulate their targets. The goal of this activity is to have students engage in a cognitive process that will enable them to recognize the "game" and decide how to handle the situation appropriately.

Teachers will need to use discretion when selecting which letters to use and how to use them. You may choose some and omit others. You may choose to delete vulgar or sexually graphic language before using the letter in class. Letters that contain sexually explicit language are labeled for easy identification.

Before using any of the grooming letters as a teaching tool, you should use Proactive Teaching (see Chapter 9) to prepare students for the content that will be covered and the skills necessary to best learn from the letters. Other suggestions for using the letters include:

- Read through all the letters before deciding which to use.

- When selecting letters, keep in mind the skill and maturity level of your students.

- To protect modesty and allow for more honest discussion, you may want to teach this unit in same-gender groups with a same-gender teacher.

- Make overhead transparencies of the letters you wish to use. **Do not make paper copies** and distribute them to students. This prevents letters from being misused or circulated outside the classroom.

- Make one copy of the Letters Answer Sheet (in Session 4) for each student to refer to during viewing and discussion of the letters.

Hey, for you I'll do it! I already talked to my dad. He said your parents are the ones doing it! My dad doesn't want us restricted! Your parents have all the power in this. I'm not in trouble, you are! It's up to you! I'll do what I can to get us less restricted. Maybe I'll talk to your parents and explain that we have never gotten into trouble before and that school is somewhere that all of our friends are at and we should not have to be restricted at least at school! Don't worry too much! Things will get better! If for some reason I'm not home tomorrow, leave a message and I'll call or come see you! I love you Boo Bear! Things will be okay! Just play it cool! Stay out of trouble! I'll do my thing and stay out of trouble too! Baby, be good and good luck! Don't forget to call! I love you!

Love always,

P.S. Have a good day. I love you. Sleep well.

Boo,

I'm sitting in class thinking of you. Tonight will be fun. I'm not sure what I'm going to wear. I'm thinking about nothing, but you might like that too much. But, I can wear a skirt for easy access! We might be able to work something out on the bus tonight!! Baby, I really love you! Seeing you makes my day! I can't wait for 3rd hour so I can see you! I don't know what I'm going to do when you go to college. It's going to be lonely! I'll always be in your heart and you in mine! Well Cream Puff, I have to work! I love you, and will definitely see you later!

Love for Always,
Me

I know me and you are best friends. I mean everything I say about you. The only thing I think you don't understand is my feelings for you. I can care less who you want, or go with. I just don't want to lose you. Sometimes I think you are being lost, or taken from me. I say, "I love you," and I mean it! All I ask is that you love me back. Talk to me about anything. You know "everything" about me, but I feel I don't know "everything" about you. Tell me.

Wuz up Sexy. Nuttin much here just sittin here thinking about what we talked about last night. I'm sorry that I started being a bitch to you. Next time I will make sure we are somewhere where I can really be a bitch. I don't know what to do anymore with you. I'm just scared that I'm gonna be the one hurt out of all this. I have a new thing we can do with chocolate. You will enjoy it. Today walk home with me. If you really want me you would do everything I ask you to. I am not upset at you because you had every reason to move on while I did my thing. I do want to be with you but I am not sure about you. You seem to want me for one thing and one thing only. If that's not true then prove me wrong.
Well I gotta bounce.

Stay Tru Blue
Lov You Real

Boo Boo –

Hey wuz up? Me not much just chillin in 5th hour waiting to go to lunch sorry for almost getting you in trouble for waiting for me. Well I am home right now and grounded. What makes me happy is smoking and drinking. I am happy with you cause I like you a lot. So what makes you happy? And how am I going to find out? I hope that soon that me and you will be happy together one day. I hope that you are happy that we go out together? Cause I am happy. I like the way that we are together you make me happy and laugh. I know that this letter is short but got to go take care.

See you later Bye

LETTER #6

To: My Baby <u>Now</u> and <u>Forever</u>

Sorry, I just want to write you. You probably don't want to hear me, but I'm writing anyway.

First, I just want to say Happy Belated Birthday again. I hope your day went better when you got home. I just wanted to let you know I love you, but I'm still going to get you. By the way, I can't go to the mall anymore. I have to stay home. I don't know if that matters to you, but it does to me. I hope you stay in a good mood, because I like it when you're in a good mood. Oh, and I hope you like my jeans, because I wore them for you! No, I just liked the style. I needed a change. Your hair cut looks cute. Gotta go.

Love ya,
Me

"Hi!" What's up? Not too much here. Please write to me what you wanted to write a.s.a.p. Just to let you know I think this relationship should start going a little faster. I think there should be some more affection. (Touching). You know affection. I wish I could just hold you forever. I love you so much. I have a few questions for you to answer –

1) Do you love me? (truly) Yes or no.
2) Do you want this relationship to go faster? Yes or no.
3) What do you think of me? (Deep down-inside your heart).
4) Do you like me touching you? Yes or no?

Peace Out. Love You.

P.S. Answer these by circling the correct answers. Thanks.

LETTER #8

Hey wuz up? I wrote you last night but I forgot the letter. So I will write you now. Last night in the letter I wrote I asked a few questions; so here they are. What do you like about me so far? What are your beliefs on touching, especially between us? Are you a virgin? Most people I would tell I have, but technically I didn't because I only got head. We almost did, but I was too messed up so I'm thankful for not doing so. But I want to let loose bad. Write back and we'll talk more. Don't let anyone read this.

To: My Husband:

Hey, hows it going? I missed you so much this weekend! You were all I could think of. I wanted to go watch you, but I couldn't. Plus, I had that stupid play I had to do. I would have talked to you last night, but my mom was watching, and she's mean. I love you! Sometimes I wonder if it is worth a detention to kiss you right in front of everyone. But, you know me, I'm paraniod! It's not that I don't want to kiss you, its that I don't want to get caught!

You know how some people say I love you and they don't mean it? Well, I do. I can't get you out of my mind. You're always there. Sometimes I just want to touch you, and make sure that you're mine. I know you are, but I like touching you anyway. There are so many things I want to do to you. A lot of the time I have the urge to just touch your chest, but I don't. I love just looking at you. And its even better because you are sweet on the inside too. Well, got ta go. WRITE ME PLEASE! I love you always and forever.

Love ya,
Me

Hey how's it going? It's going pretty good for me but your letter kinda confused me but the reason why I always look at you is because I kinda have a crush on you. You are a major cutie! And I'm sorry about pinching your nipples. I won't pinch them anymore if you don't want me to. No I don't have a boyfriend. I just broke up with one last week. I'm not sure what else to write you about. Are you going to homecoming? Do you have a date? I'm going to homecoming but I don't have a date, & I don't think anyone is gong to ask me but oh well. I'll still go and have fun. You never told me if you had a girlfriend, so do you?

Well I better go
Write me back
Love

Letter #11

Your eyes say so much and
My body want so bad to feel your touch
Gangster love
Be mine
You are so fine

I can tell you all of what you want to hear
But I'd rather you imagine
This love so strong
You see them other bitches will watch
I'll help you carry on
Breathe deeply
Cuddle up with me when you sleepy
And it doesn't even matter
Cuz what we got's fatter
Freak bitches want to match blunts
You see I laugh while they front

You and I both know
That it takes a gangster bitch
To feel my flow
And that is what helps my cash grow
What they don't do
I know

I think we need to figure out what we are going to do. I am all for getting back together but you need to make the call. You tell me what is going on. I know what I said about Jake but forget him cause I want to be with you. I have missed you so much. I really hope this works out. Why don't you talk to me after 2nd period? I want you around but you always get busy with Shawna. So did you and her have a nice talk on the phone? Talk to you later. Write back.

Hey Baby? What are you doing? I am sitting on my bed listening to my radio and thinking about you. I wish that I could give you a hug. Why do you sound so good on the phone? I like talking to you right before I go to bed because then your voice remains in my head through out the night.

I didn't mean to pry by asking if you asked Shawna to marry you. If I ever ask you something and you don't want to answer, just tell me. I wont be mad. I'm sorry about my spelling.

Any ways! I felt bad when I got to the pool and you were not there. I was happy when Todd told me that you were there finally. I think that we are alike in a lot of ways. It's weird. Well baby, I am starting to fall asleep. I love you!! I'll see you in my dreams.

Love always & forever,

LETTER #12C:

Hey, I just wanted to tell you something that I've wanted to tell you earlier. I really like you. Do you remember when I told you that I would tell you what I use to do? Well, it's later. I am known as the S.O.H. or South O Ho. I use to sleep around. I do not want you to think any less of me. I have not really liked someone since '97.' Thats when my boyfriend was killed. I have been pregnant twice but have no kids. I always got the s--- beat out of me. I have no STD's. My mom says that I am very lucky for that. Well, this is what I wanted to tell you. I also was sexually abused from the age of five to the age of eight and raped three times.

Love of my life,

Hey! How was your day? I did what you wanted me to. You know, telling my foster mom what you said to. Anyways, she said that we can talk to each other again but we cannot call each other. Babe, did I hear this right? After you finally get your baby girl back you are going to give her up for adoption. I really hope not. If this is true, I am by no means telling you what to do. I am only trying to tell you that in my point of view I don't think that it is fair to split up a family.

I am not sure if I told you or not. I have been in and out of this very messed up system. I have been in the system on & off since I was a month old. To this day I resent my mother for not keeping me or any others (my 3 brothers). One of my brothers was adopted before I was born. I hate not having normal family. Any ways, I just wanted to write so that you know that I love you and that I'm here if you need to talk. Any time day or night.

Love always,

Me

(P.S. I promise that I will not turn in any notes)

Hey Baby,

How's it going? You really don't know how much I care for you. You make me want to do things I'd <u>never</u> think of doing with anyone else. I don't know how to handle that, so I don't look at you. You honestly <u>drive me crazy</u>! I can't stop watching you, waiting for your next moves. You and that cake was about to drive me to do something…Oh well, maybe next time.

I love you <u>so</u> much, you don't even know how much. I have never cared for anyone, much less a guy, like I care for you. I want to be with you every moment of every day. I can't help waiting for the bells to ring, so I could see you. Every time you look at me I want to just kiss you. When you touch me, I want to turn around and hug you, and do other things…Sorry I can't say this to your face, but I'm really shy, believe it or not. You bring out something in me I <u>never</u> knew existed. I just don't want to get hurt, and I don't want to hurt you. I care **deeply** for you. You are one of the nicest guys I have ever met, and one of the cutest guys I've ever gone out with.

I'm not that type of person that would give it to anyone, but I think I would make a compromise for you. I want you to know I want to be with you and you alone. I hope that's the same with you. I *love* looking at you and knowing that you are mine, and that you actually like me. That means a lot to me. I have to go, but **I love you** so much it hurts. I need you, and I miss you! I love you!!

I'm thinking of you!

Love ya,

ME

LETTER #14A:

Hey Shortie,

Now I didn't get to tell you why I'm still thinking. Now I know how you get down, and there's always some other n---- that's diggin' you. So if you started talking to him while you goin wit me, everybody would have problems. But, I do want to be with you. And I know he ain't going anywhere but you just might leave. So basically I gotta trust you more. If we start talking seriously now, we could work out all of the problems and then we could be with each other. But I can't be your man now. Why did you wait so long for this. You shoulda got me when you first had a chance.

Love You,
Lil Capone

P.S. don't laugh at my name, cuz my brother gave me that!

Hey Sweety wuz ↑ or ↓ or whateva????

The reason why I didn't get wit you at first wuz cuz I wanted to get to know you better B-4 I just hooked ↑ wit you. Yeah, I know I wuz messin w/ a lotta others like C-Roc en Big Dawg. And I wuz hearin a lotta s--- bout you and 1/2 the other guys I's with. Bout how you'd cheat on me. I really wanna get wit you now because your so sweet, caring, loving and you remind me of a teddy bear that I can just cuddle with. So how do you think we can make this work? I already broke up w/C-Roc. His lil' friends hooked us up a few days ago. I never see him, we never talk and I think he's ugly anywayz. So write me back A.S.A.P. today. We'll talk later.

Stay sweet and tru lil' Capone. Why do yo Bro call you that N.E. way?

Love ya
Shortie

Shortie,

Hey, I talked to Anita and not once did she say anything about you. Yo, and you had no one call and I was supposed to go to the movies last night! Besides that, don't worry about her, because if anything is going to happen, I'll know about it before anyone else will. Besides that, she's f---n' up again, so I might just want a new girl, if you still want to. But we'll talk after school. The bell's about to ring so I gotta go!

Lil Capone

LETTER #15:

You,

Hey! I'm not for sure exactly what you want to know about me but I'll fill you in on some important things about me. <u>If</u> we get to know each other a lot better I'll tell you a lot more. Well first off I don't really get close to people unless they prove that they have a role that needs to be played in my life. I'm looking forward to getting married and having kids. I want to be a doctor or teacher. I'm a 4.0 student that doesn't know what I'm doing after HS. I love the city but the country is OK to. I'm single for the first time in my life since I was 10. I speak French, I know some Latin and Spanish. I'm part Italian, part Hispanic & Indian. I don't know anyone on my real dad's side of the family. I don't get along w/anyone on my mom's side except my mom and sisters (2) and brother. I don't get along w/ my mom's husband or his kids. I'm the oldest of 6 other kids (4 girls 2 boys). I love kids but I only want 2. I want someone to stay w/ forever. I have a high tolerance level for most anything except lying, cheating, or backstabbing. One other thing about me is I'm interested in you & so far like you a lot. Out!

♥ Me

LETTER #16:

W'sup? Not much my way just chillin.

Well I wanted to know if you have a girlfriend? Because I think your cute and if you don't do you wanna hook-up? I know we're not suppose to do this but oh, well. If you don't want to well then that's all right too. Okay. Later

P.S. Are you going to the Halloween dance?

Write back soon
Sorry so sloppy.

LETTER #17:

Dear Tanya,

I don't know you that good because I never met you. I wanted to say "I like you" when I first saw you. You made me feel special. Lucky is the guy who gets to be with a diamond like you, your eyes are so beautiful, your body, your hair. Everything. You are like candy once a guy gets a taste out of you he will go crazy.
And one day he wont taste it but eat it.

Write back.

Letter #18A:

Bumblebee,

"Love is in my heart, and in your eyes."

Hello, Love. How are ya? I'm <u>really</u> good. I'm just wondering if you saw what I mouthed to you. Well, if you didn't, I said "I love you." And I really do, too. If my love is not in the way of boyfriend, girlfriend, it's in the way that you'll always be my best friend. Please promise me nothing less than that! That tornado s--- blowed donkey nipples and raccoon tongue. I can't believe I lost sleep over that bulls---! I wish you were down there with me, where we could cuddle and fall asleep together. Oh, did I tell you that so-called "cheesy" poem was <u>very</u> cute? I try to read it every chance I get. It makes me feel so....so...I dunno...loved, maybe? Oh, I wanted to ask you why is it that you love me? Normally dudes go out with me for my looks, then they leave me finding out I'm psycho. Well, I think I'm normal, but the obsessions I have aren't normal. It's just not normal for a guy to really like me for my looks & personality. For Rod and Booker, they carried me everywhere like a trophy. All the guys at the mall wanted me, and that made me feel special. I'll tell ya more later. I gotta eat din-din. Mmmmm...food. I wish I could taste you though. I dunno which I want more – your cock or your lips....

10:04 pm

Hey, hon! I had a <u>blast!</u> Sorry I was being somewhat of a bitch @ the gym. I'm trying to not be such a liar so that the girls won't know I'm helplessly falling in love w/ you. I'm <u>not</u> having PMS!! Sorry I called you a loser. You're <u>not</u> a loser in my eyes. Not at all. Again, I was attempting to play it off.

I'm sure I confused the s--- out of you today. One minute I'm mean to you, the next minute, I'm whispering "I love you" while tapping your chest w/ my water bottle. It was all a play for the girls. If it was my choice, I'd have much rather been in your arms, probably kissing you as much as I could but it didn't end up that way. Instead, I was guilty being somewhat of a bitch to you. But you should know that I love you and care for you very much. Oh, did I tell you that it is <u>very</u> rare for me to find someone I'm sexually attracted to? Well, um…yeah, you're that rare person…oh, I was just kidding about the whole "serious relationship B.S." All of my serious relationships have turned into f--- overs, but that's not restricting me from giving you a chance. Okay? Of course I want to get married!! Who knows, you & I may end up together in holy matrimony and it'll be cool. But if we don't, I can say it was fun while it lasted. Well gotta go to sleep and dream of you! I love you.

Kanibol

Rip this up & put into TOILET, NOT TRASHCAN! FLUSH IT! Please! I ♥ U!

Hey Kiddo! So, I figured you didn't write me back. Typical dude act, so don't feel left out. Most guys don't normally write back. Ugh! I am <u>so</u> mad! But I didn't eat (If I don't eat, I get <u>really</u> crabby) and didn't put my makeup on. Normally I'm not self conscious about how

I look b/c I normally don't care what others think. <u>But</u> now that there is someone that I actually care about what they think, I almost feel I have to impress them in some way or another. Or at least look half way decent around them! So um... Yeah, I apologize for looking like s--- today. Oh – when handing me a note, do it smoothly, especially around Alicia b/c she'll rat us out. And I don't exactly feel like getting another detention. That would really suck. Did I tell you I'll miss you a lot while I'm gone? I feel weird if I go even one day w/ out seeing or talking to you. While I'm gone, I'll write to you every chance I get. Will you write to me, too? Please?!

I gotta go!

XOXOXOXO,
Kanibol

PS: Of course I'll teach you bass!

Pumpkinhead,

I am so disappointed! I can't believe you got caught last night! Obviously it was over something really stupid, huh? But oh well – I suppose I can't really control you, now can I? I wish I could – cuz then you'd be my slave! Hee hee hee hee just kidding. But seriously – you've gotta promise, pinkey swear, that while I'm gone, you'll be good and try your best to not go off, to not get mad, to control your anger and etc. PLEASE don't make me worry about you. Normally if I really start to worry about someone or something, I get sick. And being sick sucks. Just try to be good, okay? I will really miss you while I'm gone. Just be a good boy – for me.

AFTER I GOT YER NOTE

Yo-yo-yo. What is up, my homie? Un-no. Anyways. So, that was yer first note, EVER? Craziness! Why'd you set my name on fire? Are you expecting me to burn down to a million ashes? Just kidding. It's cool that yer obsessed w/ grabbing my ass.

It somewhat flatters me b/c sometimes guys like me but normally guys think I'm too f---g weird. The whole piercing and tattoo obsession grosses them out. Even Jose hates the fact I have a sick sad obsession and need for pain. He's very uncomfortable with it b/c I'd always ask him to inflict pain on me. So – yeah, it flatters me that you have (or had) a crush on me or what not. Before, I was hardcore "non-relationship." I was so in love and smitten w/Jose. I wouldn't even look @ a guy, or girl. But now I've had the time to step away and take a good look @ the relationship. I'm not one to say it'll last or not. But to the point – I think yer so-called "crush" wore off on me b/c I'm developing a slight crush on...your mom!! Just messin-on you. At least, well, I think it's a crush b/c I've never really had a "crush" before. It was always "I like you b/c you give me drugs and a place to stay." But you, I like yer personality and the way you always make me laugh. Yer a kick-ass person to be around. Well, I'll write more later, but I gotta get ready for work. See ya there and write back soon!

Kanibol

LETTER #19:

Hey honey

You asked me to write so this time I decided to actually write you. About my hair I'm sorry my hair just grows fast and I don't like it on my shoulder or on my back. It does grow to my back. So if you don't like my hair short I will grow it all out. I promise to grow it out and not cut it short!

Now you have it in writing. You ask if I was partial to gold. Well I will wear it, but it doesn't look right on me. So that's on you if you buy it or not. (I honestly don't care) I also don't know what I want for Christmas. (You get what ever you want me to have!)

I do think we can stay together unmarried. I think it will give us a chance to make up for the bored part of our relationship. I think we can wait until you finish law school and I finish medical school.

My mother asked me if I want to have you in my senior pictures. I think she does like you and I told her after graduation we will get our pictures taken. She got mad at my response and hung up on me. She'll get over it.

Love always

LETTER #20

Dear Ge Ge,

I know that your mad at me but you said that you wouldn't listen to nobody if some body told you something about me. You know if I didn't love you I would not be writing this letter. I know that when them words come out your mouth you thought I didn't care. I don't give a f--- what guys think about me and you if you don't want to come back. That's on me, you Ge Ge will steel be my girl in my heart. And that girl that came to the game with my sister to watch me play is not my girl. You are my girl and this is the last time I am going to ask you. Would you Gee be my girl. If I want to play I would of got my dick sucked by somebody else.

Yes or No
Circle and give back

Letter #21

Becca,

S---, I ain't faithful either. I mess around with everybody I haven't f---d anybody for 5 months. I need some good pussy. You got some good pussy? You think you can come to the field house tomorrow at 9:30? If I can't make it tonight, I sure can tomorrow morning.

Derrik

REPLY   Derrik,

Yes. I think I can go to the field house @ 9:30 tomorrow if you don't come tonight. I don't know what you consider good. I have only had sex once so I don't know if I'm good or not but if you tell me to do sumthen let me tell ya I'll do it. But remember keep everything on the down low.

-- Don't tell anybody
Becca

REPLY   Becca,

I'm talking about 9:30 in the morning. I have
basketball practice. I know a good place where we
can f---. I got a big dick so don't scream. I wouldn't
lie about my dick. I hope you can make it in the
morning. I want you to suck my dick, and I'll eat
your pussy. Straight up, I don't give a f---. But you
remember, don't get me caught. In the morning
tomorrow at 9:30. OK.

D.

REPLY   Big D,

When you get lonely and no one is around,
what do you do?

Becca

REPLY   B.–

"Beat my dick!" What do you do?

Big D.

REPLY   D.–

Think of how it would feel if the world was stoped
exept me and you and just dream of you sticken
your cock in my mouth and moning.

B.

LETTER #22A:

What up sexy, what's going on? Me nothing really.
I'm just sitting here grounded cuz of some fight I
had. So I'll try to call you and see what's on your
mind. Even if we don't have classes together, I still
want to see you more than I use to. You know what
I mean? I want to be closer to you than just a
boyfriend. I know this relationship will go further
than I think it will. Just by listening to you, and
looking at your nice body, and pretty eyez. I feel
you sense my mind by just even thinking about
you. And I hope this relationship lasts for a while,
or even more.

Peace: Sexy eyez

LETTER #22B:

To: My Dream Girl

From: Her Dream man

Reason: Just thinking about you

What's up girl? So anyway what you bee thinking about lately. My body all over your body is what I'm thinking about. Rub your body with mine all night and nonstop action. Smell the sex in the air, and think about it, me and you kissing under the stars on the tallest building of New York. Keep this in mind Boo, we could do anything we want in this world and all we need is each other.

P.S. I love you Girl never forget that.

LETTER #22C:

To: My Wifey

From: Her Dream Man

Reason: Just to make you wet.

What the Deal Girl? How you feeling? Well I been up to a lot lately. Every time I look at you, I see nothing but sweet f---g. Every time I look at that ass, I think about busting in it, and let the nut all over your body. I hope that pussy is fat enough. When I stick it in, you'll feel the blood rush in my vain of my dick every time I push in. I'm sorry about my sloppy handwriting, but anyways, I hope you wild as you say you are. I hope you just as true. P.S.: don't tell nobody about you know what! Call around 5:00 PM

LETTER #22D:

What's up Girl? Me nothing, just laying on my bed thinking about how some day me and you are going to be all up on each other, and one night we'll be sweating on the bed. We'll be making soo much noise that the police will start getting calls from our next door neighbors. One of these days I'm going to let you cuff my wrist soo tight, just so that you can enjoy the ride, know what mean? But I hope that you don't think f---g is all I am good for. In my life, I was known as the kid with the good dick. And girls would be all on me, just to get some, but I couldn't ignore, or resist. F---g was part of my routine. Women would only use me for that one thing. And believe it or not, I tried to look for a girl I could keep it real with. Building a relationship with a girl was impossible. Once I figured out a girl wasn't true, all I would do is f--- her, and leave in the morning. I get laid out more than I get hangovers. And that is how I thought a man supposed to be. And I still think that way. Every girl I met always had they own little ways of doing things. Some smoke and some didn't. Some would to ride and just like the legs spread action. But none of them really care about me. Every time I get arrested for some dumb s---, them girls always want to jump on someone elses dick. And every time I come back they end up pregnant. I hate girls who bulls---, and don't know what they talk about. I hope that you are not one of those girls.

LETTER #22D: (CONT.)

I would love to have a girl to feel but I also need one to talk to; talk about s--- that on our minds. Some times when I look at you I think of your lips on mine, and your long nails scratching across my back. And as I squeeze on your ass you tend to kiss and bit my lips. And how hot the room will be after I got done hitting it nice and slow. That's if that some day would happen, and I hope that some day would happen real soon in my room. I hope me and you would have something going other then just looking at each other, and having wet dreams about each other. I'm not trying to be all nasty, but it's true. If you feel like you want to smoke, let's smoke. You want to f---, lets f---. You want to bounce, and go some where lets go. Because when me and you are together, ain't nothing stopping us.

Peace Boo – And keep that pussy tight!
P.S: Meet me after school

LETTER #22E:

To: My Queen
From: her King
Reason: let you know the deal

What the deal Girl? Anything else bothering you Boo? Let me know if any motherf---a bothering you again! Somebody's ass is going to end up having a nine inch foot stuck in it. Like that bitch ass Troy. I'll wip his ass in a second. Like I said many times, once I got you wrapped round my arms, can't no one else jump in, because that chick Alisha is trying but you ain't to worry about me. Me and her used to do s--- w/ each other, but I never f---d her. I deaded her because she was going around saying I f---d her, plus she tried to f--- w/my head, and it didn't work. She had me going for a while. People told me a lot of things about how bloody her underwear was, and how her pussy was. To be honest, the reason I went out w/her was because I was desprite for some ass. As long as she giving it up I'm going to take it, but then I understood why they told me not to, because the bitch was dirty, inside and out. Before I found all this s--- out we were cool. Now, I think she still got a thing for me. So it's not just because you got a man, it's because you have me, because I not just any other man. Im amazing. Well I thought I should let you know that before we go any further, I just want to let you know that every time I look at you, I see you braging on what kind of man you got. And how wet you get every time I say I luv you.

Well Girl Ill talk to you later. Peace Boo!
I love you Girl

To: ex-wife

From: ex-man

Reason: To let you know how I'm feeling now

What the deal? I hope you don't think I hate you, just because we aint talking, I'm watching over myself. Making sure this s--- ain't gonna get any deeper. I just want to let you know that I love you and miss you too. And I try to get over you, but I can't. I've been trying to get you off my mind for a while. A lot of girl's been trying to get w/ me, but ain't none of them like you. So really, the hating type of girls won the battle. If you put yourself in my shoes, you would want to get out of them, because you wouldn't handle it. The reason why I deaded this relationship is because there was too much s--- going on. People were telling me that you and Cool D had something going on. And a lot of n---s flirt w/ you and you don't care. I still got feelings for you, but I don't want none of this other s--- happening to me. I'm getting tired so call tonite if you can.

Peace   PS: I hope you was true because
                    I always was

Hi sweet-face!

I'm supposed to be writing about science – but I want to write you! What time are you going to the game? Why do you think you would hurt me? Id ware you out before we even start to sweat! <u>You</u> would be the one screaming! I wish we could have at least one night to make love! I want to take you home w/ me tonight!, Ok? What kind of future do you want w/ me? Describe it. I want a nice house, and two cute little babies. I want to do you – your laundry – and cook your supper! I want us both to have good jobs. And a caller i.d. so I know who's calling. (I won't answer the phone.) I want to cuddle up close to you and watch t.v. every night befor we go to bed. I just want to be w/ you. Every day & night.

> I love you.
> <u>Most!</u>
> Love-your sweet-ma-ma-forever!

Smile real big!

P.S. Did you know you make other guys jelous? You must be proud. I AM!!!

LETTER #24:

Well whats up my n----??

You said we should "seperate for awhile." Well I don't want to separate. We have been going out for 1 month and a 1/2. I grew closer to you. It probably didn't seem like it. Why does it have to be like this? Baby I want to be with you. At first I was just going out with you like Boy an Girl like. But now I have real feelings for you.

I want us to be together for the rest of high school. I like you a lot and more. Cuz if not I wouldn't be writing this letter. But I aint go beg your ass to stay w/me. I wont talk to that n---- no more I won't even look at him. In case you didn't notice he is not my type. But me and him talk about more stuff then me and you ever have.

I do need some type of "social" life w/ boys cuz baby you aint giving none up. Well if you really want us to be apart let me know because some times people say stuff they don't mean when there mad.

Im saying this from the heart. No lie.

Love Ya Boo
Ya "Baby"

LETTER #25:

Girl I'm really sorry that it had to come to this...

But I'm not going home wit no f---d up kiss...

You can take this how you want

But you need to realize...

That if you wasn't selling then

You should not avertize

LETTER #26:

Dear Boo Bear,

How are you doing? Oh, I heard Santa Clause is coming to town. He called me and asked if I would do him a favor. He want me to give some guy named Boo Bear a Christmas gift. So, I've decided to do him the favor. Now, Santa told me to be creative. There are a lot of different ways to make somebody's holiday. I thought since this guy looked really hot, I'd start out with a lap dance. Then as my clothes were falling down around him I would rub whipped cream over my body. Then I would get the cherries out and suck on them. Then take off his clothes and lay him down and rub carmel all over his chocolate body. I'd lick every part of his body with my warm tongue. We would make love for hours. Then we would lay naked next to each other and play with untouchable parts of the body. I really think this would be creative! Maybe if I added hand cuffs and strawberries it would be better? What do you think? Do you think this guy would enjoy this? Santa told me to make him very happy! Let me know if you think Mr. Boo Bear would like this!! Well what else is up? I really miss you! <u>Promise</u> to call me about modern history homework! I want to hear your sexy voice and gental words!

I have to do homework now!

LETTER #27:

I just wanted to write you one last time. I'm sorry about earlier today on the phone. I was mad because everytime I decide I need to apologize or talk to you about something your parents bug out and say "NO!". I was listening to a song earlier and it goes like this:

"I want a perfect body
I want a perfect soul"

I want you to notice when I'm not around. You're so special. You're so very special.

Whatever makes you happy. Whatever you want. You're so very special. I wish I was special. But I'm a creep. I'm a whiner. What the hell am I doing here? I don't belong here!!

This is just part of how I feel about you and me. I can honestly say I know you tried your damnedest to love me and in return I gave you 5 months of hell. I know you threw the necklace out when you were mad. I feel after these three days of pain I can honestly say that I do/did love you. But I'm not going to put you through that hell again. And if that 4-5 months was hell to you just imagine experiencing the real thing up close & personal! But I just needed to get that off my chest. I still don't know what I want. Sarah said you said it was totally over and this time for good. So I respect that and just leave you saying "I LOVE YOU W/ ALL MY HEART AND I WILL ETERNALLY MISS YOU."

- Alwayz – Adidas – meaning "<u>A</u>ll <u>d</u>ay <u>I</u> <u>d</u>ream <u>a</u>bout <u>s</u>ex"
- P.S. If you want your pictures back let me know.

Hey honey,

Well you have some questions that you want me to answer so I will answer them for you.

1. My favorite color is baby blue. I don't know why it just is...

2. My favorite song is Changing Faces "Tempo"

3. My favorite meal is...(Pork --)
   No, I playing. I don't have a favorite meal, but I like Chinese food

4. On thing I regret is cheating on you.

5. The worst experience I went through is when I had a miscarriage at the age of 15.

6. The best thing I have experience is when this guy I knew asked me out on Valentine day and we stayed together for 2 yrs. He treated me like a lady and never asked me for anything in return.

7. If I could change anything I would change the relationship I have with my dad because I don't want to hate him. He just acts like an asshole and start making him choose me (his daughter) before his wife.

8. The person I trust most is Mommy and my stepdad.

9. My scariest experience was when I was held at gun point and raped. Also when I had a miscarriage, both of these night I thought I was going to die

10. The most precious thing to me is my family/my mother, brother & sister, my stepdad, yourself and Simba (he is my dog)

11. I argue the most with my birth dad and you

12. What is my greatest fantasy?? Wouldn't you like to know! At first I wasn't going to tell you, but if you really want to know I will tell you! Now don't think too much of my fantasy!

(Then goes on to a lengthy description of sexual fantasy)

PEANUT

Hey sexy how ya doin' I'm fine sorry bout what happened I know you didn't do anything but please be careful cuz I don't want you to get grounded if that happens I'll be pissed. Hey I had a hot dream about us again. Write back today if you can and I will tell about it if you want to know. It was one of the best dreams I ever had. I cant tell you now cause I'm in class. You look nice today, your hair does too. I might go to the Y tonight but I'll be swimming. I still don't see why you wont go swimin with us. If I was a girl and had a body like yours I'd be showing it off. You do have a nice body and you know it I think you'll want to know about that dream so write back and let me know.

CASPER

PEANUT

Hey what up not much here? Hey when you said you didn't want me to get hurt please don't tell me you ment by Hector. I'm not going to do anything to him but I could hurt him realy bad if we ever got in a fight. I knew I'd make you smile earlier. You have a cute smile. Yes I am your friend and no one will ever change that. Friends can fool around. I hope someday my dream does come true. You still haven't told me what you say about me to your friends. Are you goin' to the dance? I'm going and I am looking forward to seeing you tonight. I can only imagine what you will wear tonight. Well got to go. Stay fine and smiling.

CASPER

LETTER #29C:

SNOWBALL,

Hey sexy, what up? Not much here. So about that dream I had. I don't want you to look at me differently when I tell you about it. In my dream we were at a party at my house. We were there partyin' for like five hours. Later in the party you started dancing on my table. Then you jumped off the table and landed on me sittin' on the couch. You said you didn't want to get up, so we started kissin' eventually one thing led to another and we were out in my pool house having sex. In my dream you were wild. You scratched my back realy hard. If that is how you are in real life, I don't think I could handle you (Tiger) ha ha ha. Any way did you know you have a nice body? Well you do. You have nice legs. You need to show them off more. I don't see why you don't ever go swimmin'. Anyway, my dream was stupid huh. I know I shouldn't be thinkin' of you that way, but I cant help it. I'm sorry. Well I got to go. Please write me back and not a small one.

CASPER

Hey Baby,

Look, listen carefully, you want to get off this f---d up restriction this is what you, I mean we have to do. First I get off sub. Second we obey this restriction, not completely, but you know how it is now. Third you have to show them how much we care about each other and how we haven't been in trouble since we met. Next in two weeks we ask for limited restriction, a small conversation here and there, no biggie. Then as they see how we are handling it they may change. Last, oh no this should be first, go home tonight and ask whatever Family Teacher you prefer what is needed to get off restriction. And I'll talk to my Community Consultant tomorrow, and see what he thinks. Baby this is gonna work…trust me. I love you too much to be apart. This sucks and it hurts. I'm leaving 12:30 for the meet. Behave. I'll see you Monday. No I'll call Saturday. I'll ask for my break around 3:30 so it'll work. Baby I love you.

Sincerely,
Me

PS: "Be Careful."

Discussion Question Answers

Below are answers to some of the discussion questions for each of the grooming letters. You will notice that questions 1-4 are more objective in nature and are asking for certain specific responses. Questions 1-4 are designed to help students practice identifying the nine grooming tactics and elements of the grooming process as they are used in the letters. Students should respond with specific answers for each question based on the letter read. There may be more than one correct answer for each question. Below are some basic answers to questions 1-4 for each letter. Help students to see these answers and to look for more examples on their own.

You will also notice that no specific answers are provided for questions 5 and 6. No answer is provided for question 5 because the answer should always be the same. Question 5 asks, "How should you respond if you receive a letter like this?" The key word in this question is **"should."** A recipient of a grooming letter may be tempted to respond in various ways to a letter like this. However, the appropriate, healthy, and safe response would be to show the letter to an adult and ask for help, or just throw the letter away and avoid the groomer.

Question 6 asks students to think about how they would respond to a grooming letter based on who sent the letter. This question is designed to help students recognize that no matter who sent the letter, their response should generally be the same – take it to an adult and ask for help or throw it away and avoid the groomer.

LETTER #1

1. Which elements of the Grooming Process was the author using? How?

   Trust

2. Which of the nine Grooming Tactics did the author use? Give examples.

   Insecurity, control, accusations, flattery, jealousy

3. How did the author want to make the recipient feel? Give examples.

   Loved, special, insecure

4. What did the Groomer want the recipient to do?

   To follow instructions

LETTER #2

1. Which elements of the Grooming Process was the author using? How?

   Secrecy

2. Which of the nine Grooming Tactics did the author use? Give examples.

   Flattery, insecurity, bribery

3. How did the author want to make the recipient feel? Give examples.

   Sexually aroused

4. What did the Groomer want the recipient to do?

   To engage in sexual activity

Letter #3

1. Which elements of the Grooming Process was the author using? How?

   Trust

2. Which of the nine Grooming Tactics did the author use? Give examples.

   Flattery, insecurity, accusations, jealousy, and possessiveness

3. How did the author want to make the recipient feel? Give examples.

   Important

4. What did the Groomer want the recipient to do?

   To feel the same way she does

Letter #4

1. Which elements of the Grooming Process was the author using? How?

   Trust

2. Which of the nine Grooming Tactics did the author use? Give examples.

   Insecurity, bribery, anger, jealousy, intimidation, control

3. How did the author want to make the recipient feel? Give examples.

   Insecure, sexually aroused, fearful

4. What did the Groomer want the recipient to do?

   To follow instructions, be reassured

Letter #5

1. Which elements of the Grooming Process was the author using? How?

   Trust

2. Which of the nine Grooming Tactics did the author use? Give examples.

   Flattery, insecurity

3. How did the author want to make the recipient feel? Give examples.

   Obligated

4. What did the Groomer want the recipient to do?

   To continue the relationship and give the Groomer reassurance

Letter #6

1. Which elements of the Grooming Process was the author using? How?

   Trust

2. Which of the nine Grooming Tactics did the author use? Give examples.

   Flattery, insecurity, intimidation

3. How did the author want to make the recipient feel? Give examples.

   Sorry for her, flattered

4. What did the Groomer want the recipient to do?

   To come back to the relationship

LETTER #7

1. Which elements of the Grooming
    Process was the author using? How?

    Trust

2. Which of the nine Grooming Tactics
    did the author use? Give examples.

    Control, insecurity, flattery

3. How did the author want to make the
    recipient feel? Give examples.

    Insecure, fearful of relationship ending

4. What did the Groomer want the
    recipient to do?

    *To speed up the physical side of the
    relationship*

LETTER #8

1. Which elements of the Grooming
    Process was the author using? How?

    Secrecy

2. Which of the nine Grooming Tactics
    did the author use? Give examples.

    Insecurity, intimidation, control

3. How did the author want to make the
    recipient feel? Give examples.

    Sexually aroused

4. What did the Groomer want the
    recipient to do?

    *To get involved sexually, keep
    relationship private*

LETTER #9

1. Which elements of the Grooming
    Process was the author using? How?

    Trust

2. Which of the nine Grooming Tactics
    did the author use? Give examples.

    Control, flattery, intimidation

3. How did the author want to make the
    recipient feel? Give examples.

    Sexually aroused

4. What did the Groomer want the
    recipient to do?

    To give Groomer reassurance

LETTER #10

1. Which elements of the Grooming
    Process was the author using? How?

    Trust

2. Which of the nine Grooming Tactics
    did the author use? Give examples.

    *Flattery, insecurity, intimidation,
    control*

3. How did the author want to make the
    recipient feel? Give examples.

    Sexually aroused

4. What did the Groomer want the
    recipient to do?

    *To ask her to Homecoming, start a
    relationship*

Letter #11

1. Which elements of the Grooming Process was the author using? How?

   Trust

2. Which of the nine Grooming Tactics did the author use? Give examples.

   Flattery, insecurity, intimidation

3. How did the author want to make the recipient feel? Give examples.

   Sexually aroused, special

4. What did the Groomer want the recipient to do?

   To engage in sexual activity

Letter #12A

1. Which elements of the Grooming Process was the author using? How?

   Trust

2. Which of the nine Grooming Tactics did the author use? Give examples.

   Flattery, insecurity, accusations, control

3. How did the author want to make the recipient feel? Give examples.

   Flattered

4. What did the Groomer want the recipient to do?

   To resume a relationship

Letter #12B

1. Which elements of the Grooming Process was the author using? How?

   Trust

2. Which of the nine Grooming Tactics did the author use? Give examples.

   Flattery, insecurity, jealousy, possessiveness

3. How did the author want to make the recipient feel? Give examples.

   Sexually aroused, loved

4. What did the Groomer want the recipient to do?

   To have an exclusive relationship

Letter #12C

1. Which elements of the Grooming Process was the author using? How?

   Trust

2. Which of the nine Grooming Tactics did the author use? Give examples.

   Flattery, insecurity, intimidation

3. How did the author want to make the recipient feel? Give examples.

   Sorry for her

4. What did the Groomer want the recipient to do?

   To remain in the relationship out of guilt, pity, and a sense of obligation

Letter #12D

1. Which elements of the Grooming Process was the author using? How?

   Trust, secrecy

2. Which of the nine Grooming Tactics did the author use? Give examples.

   Flattery, insecurity, control

3. How did the author want to make the recipient feel? Give examples.

   Insecure, sorry for her

4. What did the Groomer want the recipient to do?

   To tell her personal information about himself, continue the relationship

Letter #13

1. Which elements of the Grooming Process was the author using? How?

   Trust

2. Which of the nine Grooming Tactics did the author use? Give examples.

   Control, flattery, insecurity

3. How did the author want to make the recipient feel? Give examples.

   Sexually aroused, obligated

4. What did the Groomer want the recipient to do?

   To stay in the relationship

Letter #14A

1. Which elements of the Grooming Process was the author using? How?

   Trust

2. Which of the nine Grooming Tactics did the author use? Give examples.

   Accusations, insecurity, intimidation

3. How did the author want to make the recipient feel? Give examples.

   Fearful

4. What did the Groomer want the recipient to do?

   To do whatever he says

Letter #14B

1. Which elements of the Grooming Process was the author using? How?

   Trust

2. Which of the nine Grooming Tactics did the author use? Give examples.

   Insecurity, accusation, control

3. How did the author want to make the recipient feel? Give examples.

   Special

4. What did the Groomer want the recipient to do?

   To begin a relationship

Letter #14C

1. Which elements of the Grooming Process was the author using? How?

    Trust

2. Which of the nine Grooming Tactics did the author use? Give examples.

    Insecurity, accusations

3. How did the author want to make the recipient feel? Give examples.

    Off balance and insecure

4. What did the Groomer want the recipient to do?

    To wait for him to decide if he wants a relationship with her

Letter #15

1. Which elements of the Grooming Process was the author using? How?

    Trust

2. Which of the nine Grooming Tactics did the author use? Give examples.

    Insecurity, flattery

3. How did the author want to make the recipient feel? Give examples.

    Unsure but special

4. What did the Groomer want the recipient to do?

    To reveal personal information

Letter #16

1. Which elements of the Grooming Process was the author using? How?

    Trust

2. Which of the nine Grooming Tactics did the author use? Give examples.

    Flattery

3. How did the author want to make the recipient feel? Give examples.

    Wanted

4. What did the Groomer want the recipient to do?

    To have sex

Letter #17

1. Which elements of the Grooming Process was the author using? How?

    Trust

2. Which of the nine Grooming Tactics did the author use? Give examples.

    Flattery

3. How did the author want to make the recipient feel? Give examples.

    Special, sexy

4. What did the Groomer want the recipient to do?

    To write back, be sexually aroused

Letter #18A

1. Which elements of the Grooming Process was the author using? How?

   Trust, secrecy

2. Which of the nine Grooming Tactics did the author use? Give examples.

   Flattery, status, intimidation, control

3. How did the author want to make the recipient feel? Give examples.

   Special, sexually aroused, wanted

4. What did the Groomer want the recipient to do?

   To be sexually aroused

Letter #18B

1. Which elements of the Grooming Process was the author using? How?

   Trust, secrecy

2. Which of the nine Grooming Tactics did the author use? Give examples.

   Control, flattery, insecurity

3. How did the author want to make the recipient feel? Give examples.

   Special, needed

4. What did the Groomer want the recipient to do?

   To write back, not get her in trouble

Letter #18C

1. Which elements of the Grooming Process was the author using? How?

   Trust

2. Which of the nine Grooming Tactics did the author use? Give examples.

   Control, intimidation, flattery

3. How did the author want to make the recipient feel? Give examples.

   Liked, special

4. What did the Groomer want the recipient to do?

   To like her, write her, not get in trouble

Letter #19

1. Which elements of the Grooming Process was the author using? How?

   Trust

2. Which of the nine Grooming Tactics did the author use? Give examples.

   Control, bribery, intimidation

3. How did the author want to make the recipient feel? Give examples.

   In charge, special, sexually aroused

4. What did the Groomer want the recipient to do?

   To stay in the relationship

LETTER #20

1. Which elements of the Grooming
    Process was the author using? How?

    Trust

2. Which of the nine Grooming Tactics
    did the author use? Give examples.

    Intimidation, control

3. How did the author want to make
    the recipient feel? Give examples.

    Threatened, special

4. What did the Groomer want the
    recipient to do?

    To give him a second chance

LETTER #21 (SERIES)

1. Which elements of the Grooming
    Process were the authors using? How?

    Secrecy

2. Which of the nine Grooming Tactics
    did the author use? Give examples.

    Control, bribery, status, intimidation

3. How did the author want to make
    the recipient feel? Give examples.

    Sexually aroused, intimidated

4. What did the Groomer want the
    recipient to do?

    To have a sexual encounter

LETTER #22A

1. Which elements of the Grooming
    Process was the author using? How?

    Trust

2. Which of the nine Grooming Tactics
    did the author use? Give examples.

    Flattery

3. How did the author want to make
    the recipient feel? Give examples.

    Wanted, special

4. What did the Groomer want the
    recipient to do?

    To get close sexually

LETTER #22B

1. Which elements of the Grooming
    Process was the author using? How?

    Trust

2. Which of the nine Grooming Tactics
    did the author use? Give examples.

    Flattery, intimidation

3. How did the author want to make
    the recipient feel? Give examples.

    Sexually aroused, needed

4. What did the Groomer want the
    recipient to do?

    To have sex

Letter #22C

1. Which elements of the Grooming Process was the author using? How?

   Secrecy

2. Which of the nine Grooming Tactics did the author use? Give examples.

   Intimidation, flattery, control, anger

3. How did the author want to make the recipient feel? Give examples.

   Sexually aroused

4. What did the Groomer want the recipient to do?

   To keep it secret, have sex

Letter #22D

1. Which elements of the Grooming Process was the author using? How?

   Trust

2. Which of the nine Grooming Tactics did the author use? Give examples.

   Flattery, intimidation, anger, control

3. How did the author want to make the recipient feel? Give examples.

   Sexually aroused

4. What did the Groomer want the recipient to do?

   To have sex with him

Letter #22E

1. Which elements of the Grooming Process was the author using? How?

   Trust

2. Which of the nine Grooming Tactics did the author use? Give examples.

   Status, intimidation, anger, insecurity

3. How did the author want to make the recipient feel? Give examples.

   Scared, protected, sexually aroused

4. What did the Groomer want the recipient to do?

   To have sex

Letter #22F

1. Which elements of the Grooming Process was the author using? How?

   Trust

2. Which of the nine Grooming Tactics did the author use? Give examples.

   Flattery, intimidation, status

3. How did the author want to make the recipient feel? Give examples.

   Loved, special, sorry for him

4. What did the Groomer want the recipient to do?

   To get back together with him

Letter #23

1. Which elements of the Grooming Process was the author using? How?

   Trust

2. Which of the nine Grooming Tactics did the author use? Give examples.

   Intimidation, control, flattery, status

3. How did the author want to make the recipient feel? Give examples.

   Sexually aroused

4. What did the Groomer want the recipient to do?

   To have sex, live with her

Letter #24

1. Which elements of the Grooming Process was the author using? How?

   Trust

2. Which of the nine Grooming Tactics did the author use? Give examples.

   Jealousy, control, intimidation, insecurity

3. How did the author want to make the recipient feel? Give examples.

   Threatened

4. What did the Groomer want the recipient to do?

   To have sex

Letter #25

1. Which elements of the Grooming Process was the author using? How?

   Trust

2. Which of the nine Grooming Tactics did the author use? Give examples.

   Intimidation, control, insecurity

3. How did the author want to make the recipient feel? Give examples.

   Threatened

4. What did the Groomer want the recipient to do?

   To have sex

Letter #26

1. Which elements of the Grooming Process was the author using? How?

   Trust

2. Which of the nine Grooming Tactics did the author use? Give examples.

   Flattery, intimidation, bribery, control

3. How did the author want to make the recipient feel? Give examples.

   Sexually aroused

4. What did the Groomer want the recipient to do?

   To have sex

Letter #27

1. Which elements of the Grooming Process was the author using? How?

   Trust

2. Which of the nine Grooming Tactics did the author use? Give examples.

   Anger, intimidation, insecurity, flattery

3. How did the author want to make the recipient feel? Give examples.

   Special, sorry for her

4. What did the Groomer want the recipient to do?

   To resume the relationship

Letter #28

1. Which elements of the Grooming Process was the author using? How?

   Trust

2. Which of the nine Grooming Tactics did the author use? Give examples.

   Insecurity, bribery

3. How did the author want to make the recipient feel? Give examples.

   Sexually aroused

4. What did the Groomer want the recipient to do?

   To have sex, like her

Letter #29A

1. Which elements of the Grooming Process was the author using? How?

   Secrecy

2. Which of the nine Grooming Tactics did the author use? Give examples.

   Accusations, flattery, insecurity

3. How did the author want to make the recipient feel? Give examples.

   Sexually aroused

4. What did the Groomer want the recipient to do?

   To have sex

Letter #29B

1. Which elements of the Grooming Process was the author using? How?

   Trust

2. Which of the nine Grooming Tactics did the author use? Give examples.

   Anger, intimidation, control, flattery

3. How did the author want to make the recipient feel? Give examples.

   Sexy, scared

4. What did the Groomer want the recipient to do?

   To have a sexual encounter

Letter #29C

1. Which elements of the Grooming
   Process was the author using? How?

   Trust

2. Which of the nine Grooming Tactics
   did the author use? Give examples.

   Flattery, intimidation

3. How did the author want to make the
   recipient feel? Give examples.

   Sexy, desirable

4. What did the Groomer want the
   recipient to do?

   To have sex

Letter #30

1. Which elements of the Grooming
   Process was the author using? How?

   Trust

2. Which of the nine Grooming Tactics
   did the author use? Give examples.

   Control

3. How did the author want to make the
   recipient feel? Give examples.

   Special, loved, under his control

4. What did the Groomer want the
   recipient to do?

   *To follow his instructions and break
   the rules so that they can be together*

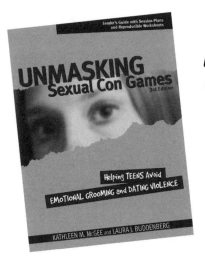